FROM THE LIBRARY OF
AJO

Praise for Jason Zweig's

THE DEVIL'S FINANCIAL DICTIONARY

"This is the most amusing presentation of the principles of finance that I have ever seen."

— **Robert J. Shiller**, professor of finance, Yale University;
Nobel laureate in economics; author of *Irrational Exuberance*

"Someone had to write a short, punchy book on the fibs and fables of Wall Street during this second Gilded Age for the extravagantly-paid manipulators of our financial system. Happily for readers— whether wise, naïve, or victimized—journalist Jason Zweig picked up the challenge, and ran for the winning touchdown with it. Laugh, cry, and learn as you enjoy the sparkling *Devil's Financial Dictionary*."

— **John C. Bogle**, founder of The Vanguard Group;
author of *Common Sense on Mutual Funds*

"A delightfully humorous and stunningly irreverent Ambrose Bierce for financial markets. This satirical critique of what passes for wisdom on Wall Street belongs on the bookshelf of every serious investor."

— **Burton G. Malkiel**, professor of finance emeritus, Princeton
University; author of *A Random Walk Down Wall Street*

"Open this wonderful book to any page. Try not to laugh. I dare you."

— **James Grant**, *Grant's Interest Rate Observer*

"Jason Zweig's book is absolutely marvelous. It combines wicked humor, scholarly etymology, and superb advice. If you have money invested, you must read this book; if you don't, read it anyway for pure fun."

— **William F. Sharpe**, emeritus professor of finance, Stanford
University; Nobel laureate in economics

"You'll love this book. Zweig cuts through financial hypocrisy to expose Wall Street's cynical core, and does it hilariously. You'll also get some super-smart investment tips. One of my favorite devilish definitions: 'Broker: Buys and sells stocks, bonds, mutual funds, and other assets for people who are under the delusion that the broker is doing something other than guesswork.'"

—**Jane Bryant Quinn**, author of *Making the Most of Your Money Now*

"Both witty and wise—with just a refreshing dash of cynicism—*The Devil's Financial Dictionary* should be on every desk on both Wall Street and Main Street."

—**John Steele Gordon**, author of *An Empire of Wealth* and *The Business of America*

"Vintage Jason Zweig: entertaining, truthful and oh so telling about Wall Street. The definition of Day Trader—'*n. See IDIOT.*'—says it all. Any investor who does not read this witty, insightful and rueful reminder of Wall Street's financial follies is an IDIOT!"

—**Consuelo Mack**, anchor and executive producer, Consuelo Mack WealthTrack

"Jason Zweig has long been a brilliant financial journalist. People who have listened to Jason have shielded their assets from the purveyors of costly and useless advice. In *The Devil's Financial Dictionary*, Jason turns his wit and insight to arming us with an understanding of the financial terms that too many professionals use to intentionally baffle investors."

—**Max H. Bazerman,** co-director, the Center for Public Leadership, John F. Kennedy School of Government, Harvard University; author of *The Power of Noticing*

"Broad experience, thorough conversance with history, unusual insight, and dashes of humor and cynicism. This is what you need to understand the world of investing, and this is what you'll find in *The Devil's Financial Dictionary* by Jason Zweig."

—**Howard Marks**, co-chairman, Oaktree Capital Management, L.P.; author, *The Most Important Thing: Uncommon Sense for the Thoughtful Investor*

"Jason Zweig, one of the great truth-tellers in financial journalism, is the spiritual heir to Ambrose Bierce, one of the great satirists in American letters. Both use piercing wit to reveal important truths."

—**Gary Belsky**, coauthor of *Why Smart People Make Big Money Mistakes and How to Correct Them*

"Wall Street frequently uses complex terminology to keep its own customers in the dark. That is why Jason Zweig's *The Devil's Financial Dictionary* is so refreshing. Zweig, who has a lifetime of experience covering finance, exposes the language of Wall Street with sharp wit, historical perspective, and a skeptic's eye."

—**Tadas Viskanta**, founder and editor, Abnormal Returns; author of *Abnormal Returns: Winning Strategies from the Frontlines of the Investment Blogosphere*

"THE DEVIL'S FINANCIAL DICTIONARY, n. A compendium of financial jargon observed to induce in its readers nearly continuous spasms of raucous laughter. Has also been known to produce near-fatal episodes of cognitive dissonance in brokers, advisors, and money managers, who should consume its contents with care. Normal individuals, in contrast, may incur a deepening of financial wisdom, a fattening of the wallet, and an uncontrollable urge to steal entire passages for later use."

—**William J. Bernstein**, author of *The Four Pillars of Investing* and *A Splendid Exchange*

"If finance were stand-up comedy, Jason Zweig would be its Groucho Marx—a serious man with a wild sense of humor: 'Dog: A stock that obeys no command except DOWN.' Need I say more?"

—**Laurence B. Siegel**, research director, CFA Institute Research Foundation

"'Witty' and 'fun' are two adjectives that may never have been used to describe a dictionary, but they apply to this one. But it is not just jokes; I learned a lot browsing around in this clever little book."

—**Richard H. Thaler**, professor of behavioral science and economics, University of Chicago Booth School of Business; author of *Misbehaving* and coauthor of *Nudge*

"Cynical and exceptionally witty, this book shines a light into the unlit corners of finance. After a lot of laughs, I walked away with a less distorted view of reality."

—**Shane Parrish**, CEO of Farnam Street Media

"Jason Zweig is a journalist known for his wise investment counsel. But he also has a wicked wit, which is on full display in *The Devil's Financial Dictionary*. A fun romp for those who don't take themselves too seriously."

—**Michael J. Mauboussin**, head of global financial strategies, Credit Suisse; author of *The Success Equation* and *Think Twice*

"Fun, interesting, irreverent, and well-informed, Jason Zweig scores again. You'll laugh and cry—and send copies to your friends."

—**Charles D. Ellis**, founder, Greenwich Associates; author of *Winning the Loser's Game: Timeless Strategies for Successful Investing*

"Finally, in language every investor can understand, *The Devil's Financial Dictionary* lays waste to the hubris of Wall Street. The definition of INDEX FUND should be read over and over again.

—**Gregory Berns**, distinguished professor of neuroeconomics, Emory University; author, *Iconoclast* and *How Dogs Love Us*

"I tried to write definitions wittier than Jason Zweig's but couldn't. Instead, I laughed, chuckled, and chortled through the book. I bet you will too."

—**Meir Statman**, professor of finance, Santa Clara University; author of *What Investors Really Want*

THE DEVIL'S
FINANCIAL
DICTIONARY

THE DEVIL'S
FINANCIAL
DICTIONARY

JASON ZWEIG

PublicAffairs
New York

Front endpapers: "Avaritia (Greed)," Pieter van der Heyden after
Pieter Bruegel the Elder, engraving, 1558. Rijksmuseum

Back endpapers: "Invidia (Envy)," Pieter van der Heyden after Pieter
Bruegel the Elder, engraving, 1558. Rijksmuseum

Published in the United States by PublicAffairs™,
a Member of the Perseus Books Group

PublicAffairs books are available at special discounts for bulk purchases
in the US by corporations, institutions, and other organizations. For more
information, please contact the Special Markets Department at the Perseus
Books Group, 2300 Chestnut Street, Suite 200, Philadelphia, PA 19103,
call (800) 810-4145, ext. 5000, or e-mail special.markets@perseusbooks.com.

Book Design by Pauline Brown

Library of Congress Cataloging-in-Publication Data
Zweig, Jason.
    The devil's financial dictionary / Jason Zweig. — First Edition.
        pages   cm
    ISBN 978-1-61039-699-8 (hardback) — ISBN 978-1-61039-606-6
(e-book) 1. Finance—United States—Dictionaries. 2. Stock exchanges—
United States—Dictionaries. 3. Finance—United States—Humor. 4. Stock
exchanges—United States—Humor. I. Title.
HG185.U6Z94 2015
332.02'07—dc23   2015015109

First Edition

10 9 8 7 6 5 4 3 2

For my father,
who knew everything,
including when not to be cynical.

INTRODUCTION:
DID THE DEVIL
MAKE THEM DO IT?

WE ARE LIVING IN A LATTER-DAY GILDED AGE, AND MUCH of what glitters is fool's gold.

Millions of ordinary investors lost trillions of dollars when stock and bond markets crashed in 2008, largely because the world's biggest banks, brokerages, and other financial companies gorged on reckless risks. Like Mr. Creosote, the character in Monty Python's *The Meaning of Life* who shovels mountains of food down his gullet until he explodes, Wall Street refused to acknowledge that enough was enough. After stuffing themselves and their clients full of dodgy mortgages at bogus prices with shoddy assertions of safety, many of the world's biggest banks toppled when housing prices fell.

Meanwhile, financial executives whose irresponsible policies and slipshod oversight contributed to the collapse nevertheless earned—and kept—billions of dollars in bonuses, stock options, and other forms of incentive compensation. Many of them are still basking in baronial splendor, apparently unscathed even by the pangs of guilty conscience.

During the first Gilded Age of the late nineteenth century, the great American satirist Ambrose Bierce assembled

"The Fat Kitchen," Pieter van der
Heyden after Pieter Bruegel the Elder,
engraving, 1563. RIJKSMUSEUM

his masterpiece, *The Devil's Dictionary*. Born in 1842, largely self-educated, a Civil War veteran who had come face-to-face with Satan on the battlefields of Shiloh and Chickamauga, Bierce was a ferocious enemy of euphemism, hypocrisy, and muddleheaded thinking. His dictionary, which he wrote in installments over the course of decades and finally published in book form in 1906, scoured the artificial gleam off nearly every institution and pretension of that opulent era.

As a financial journalist since 1987, I don't believe that Wall Street is evil. (I use "Wall Street" as a synonym for the financial industry, wherever it is situated.) There's no doubt that a minority of people in finance knowingly defrauded the public. But inattention, complacency, and overconfidence contributed far more to the financial crisis than dishonesty did. The thousands of people I have met over the years in banking, investment, and finance are predominantly honest, hardworking, decent, generous, and intelligent. And, fortunately for them if they read this book, they can laugh at themselves.

But, like most human beings, people in the financial industry are better at rationalizing than at being rational. Even as they are skidding down the slippery slope of putting their own interests first, they can readily justify every action as being in the service of a higher calling. It becomes much easier to fool other people once you have fooled yourself into believing that what you are doing is right—and, as the physicist Richard Feynman warned, "You are the easiest person to fool."

If investors are to be partners instead of pigeons, they must master the many ways in which Wall Street uses language to conceal rather than reveal information. Every profession is a conspiracy against the laity, and every profession's jargon is meant to confuse and exclude those who aren't part of the guild. Turning words inside out to make them mean the opposite isn't unique to Wall Street; it is the hallmark of the lingo in many fields, as personified by the Ministry of Truth in George Orwell's novel *Nineteen Eighty-Four*.

But rarely is so much at stake in the clear understanding of language: if you find yourself fooled by Wall Street's gibberish and buy the wrong investment, your dream of a prosperous retirement can be reduced to dust.

So this book seeks to distill the complexities, obscurities, and pomposities of Wall Street into pithy definitions anyone can understand. It is thus a survival guide to the hostile wilderness of the financial markets, where the grammatically challenged motto I once saw emblazoned on the back of a taxi in Sierra Leone is the perfect warning to anyone who tries to invest without understanding the odds: "God Help Those Who Help Themselves." You cannot help yourself unless you have at least a basic understanding of the claptrap and gobbledygook that dominate the vocabulary of the typical banker, broker, or financial advisor.

The definitions here cover a wide range of business and financial knowledge, from accounting and corporate finance to behavioral economics, investment management, and technical analysis—everything that an intelligent investor or consumer of business information would want to know.

A few themes run in common through many different entries:

𝓎 Luck, uncertainty, and surprise are the most fundamental physical forces in the world of investing. Wall Street's communications with the rest of the world are often designed specifically to deny the power of these forces.

𝓎 The denser the jargon, and the more polysyllabic the terminology, the more likely someone is hiding something from you. Words like *algorithm* and *proprietary* and *quantitative* are meant to lull listeners into a kind of befuddled surrender. (Throw them together to get *proprietary quantitative algorithm* and you have a phrase that you can launch at the brain of a novice investor like a barrage of heavy artillery.) The way to a man's heart may be through his stomach, but the way to pick an investor's pocket is through the ear.

𝓎 The financial past doesn't repeat itself exactly, but it rhymes. Human nature never changes, no matter how vociferously someone tries to tell you that this time is different. Fads come and go, but fees are forever. On Wall Street, *everything* has been tried before. Whatever it is, it will almost certainly turn out the same this time as last time.

𝓎 Sooner or later—often sooner than anyone expects—what has gone up will come down. Likewise, whatever has gone down will rise again, typically when the experts least expect it to.

𝓎 Wall Street sells stocks and bonds, but what it really peddles is hope. The investing public wants to believe in magic, and the financial industry profits from staffing an endless parade of people who claim to know the future and to be able to perform miracles. Whatever you do, don't follow the procession.

℣ Achieving financial success isn't about defeating professionals at their game. It's about achieving self-control, so you can step back from both the euphoria and the despair that alternately seize the financial markets every few years.

Throughout his *Devil's Dictionary*, Ambrose Bierce sprinkled poetry, proverbs, and anecdotes attributed to imaginary characters with such peculiar names as Mumfrey Mappel, Hassan Brubuddy, Apuleius M. Gokul, Dr. Jamrach Holobom, and a prolific Jesuit poet christened Gassalasca Jape.

In the same spirit, *The Devil's Financial Dictionary* also includes flights of fancy that are set off from the rest of the text by a red 💲. I made up these people and their words; they aren't real, I swear.

Like Bierce's entries, the definitions presented here should not—quite—be taken as literally true. But most of them are very close; no matter how cynical you are about Wall Street, you aren't cynical enough. And the Devil must know his way around the financial world, because every once in a while it does his bidding.

AAA, *adj.* Traditionally pronounced "triple-A"—but, more recently, "AAAAAAAAAAAAAAAAAAAAAGH!"

AAA is a grade assigned to a SECURITY by a RATING AGENCY such as Standard & Poor's, Moody's, or Fitch, indicating that it is "highest quality" and has "the lowest expectation of DEFAULT risk." Even so, in 2007–2009, thousands of securities rated AAA turned out to be lowest quality with the highest default risk. In the first three quarters of 2008, more than 11,000 issues of AAA rated mortgage-related securities had their ratings abruptly downgraded. The prices of many fell 70 percent or more; investors lost hundreds of billions of dollars.

See also CREDIT RATING.

ACCOUNT, *n.* The money you have at a brokerage, investment advisor, bank, or other firm, subject to continuous and sudden change from income, profits, losses, and fees. The firm will use a monthly or quarterly ACCOUNT STATEMENT to call maximum attention to the income or profits while minimizing or disguising the losses and fees.

The word has several alternate meanings. "To account" is to tell a story, particularly in order to justify one's actions. "To call to account" or "bring to account" means to make a steward responsible for what has happened, especially if the outcome was harmful. "The final account" is God's ultimate rendering of justice on the Day of Judgment.

The first of those alternate meanings is retained in the modern financial usage of "account." The others have conveniently been forgotten.

"Account" is also a slang term for CLIENT:

$ *"This gentleman is my best account," said Moe DiNero, a wealth manager at the brokerage firm of Blitz, Baum & Newcombe in Eureka, California, pointing to a name on his computer screen. "I earn more fees off him than I do off anybody else."*

ACCOUNT STATEMENT, n. A document from a bank, brokerage, or investment firm that is designed to be incomprehensible to CLIENTS, thereby preventing them from asking impertinent questions like "Who set my money on fire?" You might be able to recognize your balances and recent transactions on an account statement, although that will be easier if you earn a PhD in cryptography first.

ACCUMULATE, v.; **ACCUMULATION**, n. A term often used by ANALYSTs to recommend a stock without uttering the word "buy," thereby enabling them to duck at least some blame if the stock later collapses.

$ *"Why did you recommend buying Vertiginous Corp. at its all-time high?"* asked an angry client. *"I lost 88 percent in a week!"*

Kent B. Thoreau, a senior analyst at the brokerage firm Schmutz, Garbisch, Dreck & Pugh, responded calmly, "I didn't recommend buying it, I recommended accumulating it."

ACQUISITION, *n.* A transaction in which one company pays too much to buy another.

As Warren Buffett wrote, "If a CEO is enthused about a particularly foolish acquisition, both his internal staff and his outside advisors will come up with whatever projections are needed to justify his stance. Only in fairy tales are emperors told that they are naked."

ACT, *v.* What a financial market supposedly does, as if it were a living creature with a sense of self and volition. Traders and market analysts will say "the market isn't acting right," or "the market is acting like it wants to go up no matter what," or "the market is acting nervous." Research led by Michael Morris, a social psychologist at Columbia University, shows that investors are more likely to expect a market trend to continue when stock-price changes are likened to physical actions.

Such active images as "the Dow fought its way upward today" or "the market broke free and climbed higher" impart a power of their own. People are inherently excited by motion—especially when it is described in terms familiar from our social interactions. Depicting a financial market as an athlete sprinting, leaping, and cliff diving makes news coverage much more exciting than a droning flux of numbers.

And the belief that markets "act" is centuries old. In seventeenth-century Amsterdam, stocks were called *actie*, or "actions," and a trader was known as an *actionist*; in France, traders were called *actionnaires*.

That doesn't make the belief valid, however. A market that is "leaping up 20 points" might seem more likely to keep going up than a market that "has gone up 20 points," but it isn't. Millions of traders are squaring off, and no one can sell unless someone else is buying. The stock market isn't a unified force and doesn't act in unison; it is a mechanism that enables people with opposing opinions to put a price on their differences. Investors should therefore ignore any verbs used to describe how the market is "acting." Instead, ask how large the price change is in percentages. Chances are, a leaping or surging or racing or plunging or collapsing or diving market has barely moved by even 1 percent.

ACTIVE, *adj.* A stock is *active* when trading is high— typically generating wealth for the brokers who execute the trades and destroying it for the people who request the trades.

PORTFOLIO MANAGERs are *active* when they seek to beat the market by identifying the best investments and avoiding the worst. To do so, the managers study the investments so exhaustively that by the time they understand them, the information has become outdated and they have to sell them. That takes most managers approximately one year and costs investors 1 percent to 2 percent of their wealth annually.

Several studies have shown that if active managers did nothing all year, they would increase their performance by approximately 1 percentage point. Thus, fund managers would likely improve their performance if they went on a yearlong vacation on January 1 or replaced themselves with potted ficus trees. But it isn't easy to market yourself that way, so active managers persist in destroying wealth instead of creating it—at least for their clients.

See also FEE; PORTFOLIO TURNOVER; RESEARCH.

ACTIVIST, *n.* Known as "holdup artists" in the 1920s and "corporate raiders" in the 1980s, these agitators seek to profit by shaking up an underperforming company, typically by buying a large block of shares and then demanding that DIVIDENDs be raised, assets sold, or MANAGEMENT fired. Now that pension funds and other SOPHISTICATED INVESTORs back their efforts with billions of dollars, these dealmakers go by the more dignified name of "activists."

AFFINITY FRAUD, *n.* A financial crime committed by someone with an affinity for doing terrible things to his friends, as when a crook promotes a bogus investment to members of his church, social club, ethnic group, or other close-knit community. They trust him because they know him so well. In return, he trusts them not to notice that he is stealing their money.

ALGO, *n.* Short for ALGORITHMIC TRADER or ALGORITHMIC TRADING, in which computers substitute the risks of mechanical, electronic error for the risks of human, emotional error. Much of the time, that is an improvement, but when it goes wrong it can lead to a FLASH CRASH. Using the tools of HIGH-FREQUENCY TRADING, algos buy and sell automatically, at high speed and often in tiny increments, roving from market to market, moment to moment, to sniff out the best price. An order to sell 10,000 shares, for instance, might slice that block into tiny pieces, selling 47 shares at the New York Stock Exchange at 10:01:52 A.M. for $37.88, 56 shares at the NASDAQ exchange at 10:01:53 A.M. for $37.89, and so on. The algo will continue the instruction to sell until all the shares have been liquidated, which could take anywhere from a few seconds to a few days. If all the algos sell at once, however, trillions of dollars may be torched in a matter of seconds.

ALLIGATOR SPREAD, n. A trade in the OPTIONs market that generates such carnivorous commissions that the person who places the trade stands no chance of making a profit. (Related terms are *Acapulco spread*, *Midas spread*, and *Cadillac spread*, all nicknamed for their ability to fund lavish spending by the broker who earns them from clients.)

ALPHA, n. Luck.

Technically, *alpha* is the excess return over a market INDEX, adjusted for the risk that the PORTFOLIO MANAGER incurred to achieve it. Used as a synonym for *skill*, alpha is in fact nearly always the result of random chance:

 $ *"We bought Mongolian mortgage-backed securities when other investors had decided that the market for yurts would collapse," said Ivana Butler, an analyst at the investment-management firm Bosch, Tosh & Mullarkey in Boston. "But an outbreak of botulism among camels and yaks sent the yurt market higher, driving up the price of our bonds. This is only the latest example of the alpha-generating research process that enables us to outperform."*

AMORTIZE, *v.* To liquidate or eliminate a debt through periodic payments; also, to spread an expense evenly across a period of time until it goes to zero. Rooted in the Latin *mortuus,* meaning "dead," to amortize means literally to kill. Even brain cells can be amortized when the effects of time on money are described:

$ *"Yes, 5.75 percent might seem like a lot to pay up front for a mutual fund," said Hannah Dover, a financial advisor at the Chicago-based brokerage firm Stoneham, Black & Blue. "But when you amortize that over the next twenty-five years, it's only 0.23 percent per year, which is a bargain price for access to my advice for the next quarter of a century."*

AMPHIVENA, *n.* Also: **AMPHISBAENA,** *n.* An obscure mythical creature long believed to exist only in ancient and medieval bestiaries, the amphivena has one head at the end of a long neck and

Detail from a thirteenth-century English illuminated manuscript.
THE BRITISH LIBRARY

another at the end of a long tail. Far from being imaginary or extinct, the amphivena has materialized, in the modern era, as those "on-the-one-hand-on-the-other-hand" creatures known as ECONOMISTs and MARKET STRATEGISTs.

The amphivena is traditionally described as being able to move both forward and backward, or to rock back and forth on its round stomach. Fortunately, the amphivena most often strikes out at itself. The creature was often portrayed with one head gnawing away at the other, or with neck and tail entangled in dubious battle with each other—postures familiar today to anyone who has watched an economist or market strategist being interviewed on television.

ANALYST, n. A purported expert on a company who in theory estimates its value by breaking it down into its constituent parts but in practice functions as a salesperson and cheerleader.

    💲 *"We think CyberSushi will earn $1.43 per share this quarter," said Rosie C. Nareo, an analyst at Merck, Mudd, Marsh & Meyer, a brokerage firm in Muscle Shoals, Alabama, who follows the fast-growing company, which distributes raw fish over tablet computers. "I talk almost every day with management, and I've never heard them so optimistic."*

ANCHORING, n. A mental shortcut, or HEURISTIC, that automatically seizes upon a readily available number, no matter how irrelevant, as the basis for estimating a value or probability, thus stopping the human mind from wandering too far in search of new evidence. In one common form of anchoring, analysts often set "price targets" far above or below the market price of a security. The numbers then lodge in the mind of any investor who encounters them, serving as anchors to drag expectations toward them, regardless of how ridiculous they are.

> $ *In an appearance yesterday on the financial television network CNBS, analyst Gilda Lilly of the Atlanta investment bank Fuller Bologna said, "We think SnapAppCapp could be worth $1,000 a share six months from now." SnapAppCapp Corp., the company that enables teenagers to send and receive text messages through their baseball caps, recently traded around $150. "You'd have to be crazy to think it could go up that much," said Roland E. Dice, an individual investor in St. Louis, Missouri, who says he "plays" the market. "I mean, sure, maybe it could, like, double from here. That'd be only $300. But $1,000? That's absurd."*

ANNUAL MEETING, *n.* A yearly gathering at a hotel serving bad food and stale coffee, somewhere near an airport, at which the company's management gilds its results and pretends to listen to the wishes and grievances of the people who own the company.

ANNUAL REPORT, *n.* A yearly embellishment of a company's financial condition, featuring glossy pictures of smiling employees and customers, burnished images of the company's goods and services, and many pages of financial information presented to be as opaque and confusing as possible. The detailed version of an annual report, the 10-K, is more useful: its footnotes often explain how a company is trying to hide its accounting shenanigans.

As Peter Lynch, the renowned manager of the Fidelity Magellan Fund, wrote, "It's no surprise why so many annual reports end up in the garbage can. The text on the glossy pages is the understandable part, and that's generally useless, and the numbers in the back are incomprehensible, and that's supposed to be important."

In the nineteenth century, corporate bylaws often forbade outsiders from even examining the financial statements of the companies they invested in. Not until 1933 did the New York Stock Exchange require listed companies to have their annual financial statements prepared by an independent auditor. The history of companies hiding or cloaking the facts is much longer than the history of them disclosing it, so no investor should be surprised at the opacity of any annual report.

ANNUITY, n. From the Latin *annuus,* or yearly; an investment that often provides a regular annual income for its buyers but always does for its sellers.

ANOMALY, n. An investing strategy or valuation technique that generates a higher return than the market without obviously higher risk and thus cannot be explained in the context of EFFICIENT MARKET HYPOTHESIS. The JANUARY EFFECT is one example. Every year, several new anomalies are trumpeted in articles published in academic journals. Soon after the results of their past outperformance are published, anomalies tend to begin

THE DEVIL'S FINANCIAL DICTIONARY   11

underperforming—partly because of REGRESSION TO THE MEAN, partly because new money rushes into the approach and eliminates any remaining potential for extra return, partly because flesh-and-blood investors incur taxes and trading costs that a professor's spreadsheets never have to pay, and partly because the results might have been nothing but a statistical fluke.

As the Nobel Prize–winning economist Merton Miller put it, "Above-normal profits, wherever they are found, inevitably carry with them the seeds of their own decay."

Anomaly derives from the ancient Greek for "irregular" or "uneven"; investors should bear that original meaning in mind whenever they consider investing on the basis of an anomaly.

APOLOGY, *n.* In the real world, an admission of culpability and remorse for an action that harmed someone else, typically followed by an attempt to right the wrong and a commitment not to repeat it; on Wall Street, a declaration that *other people* did something wrong and that any resulting harm was caused by circumstances beyond the bank's control. A Wall Street apology always purports to take responsibility, but usually omits contrition, shame, a desire to make good on what went bad, or the willingness to make sure the same behavior never happens again.

💲 *In testimony at congressional hearings today, Manuel B. Schacht, chief executive of Bellow, Blair, Howell, Huff & Bragg, the investment bank, apologized for the $794 billion in losses his firm incurred on securities backed by the value of beachfront property*

in the Central African Republic. "I accept full respon-
sibility for what happened, and as a firm we deeply
regret the inconvenience that investors and taxpayers
have experienced," said Mr. Schacht.

He added: "The worst of the suffering, however, will
be borne by our own employees, who must forgo their fu-
ture bonuses and search for work elsewhere while bearing
the stigma now so unfairly attached to our firm. It is im-
portant for policymakers and the public to recognize that,
while mistakes were made, these losses were triggered by
events beyond our control."

ARM'S LENGTH, *adj.* Purportedly executed on the same terms that would have applied if the two sides in a negotiation or deal had no affiliation with each other. For example, a company may hire one of its retired executives to do consulting work in an "arm's-length transaction." Whether the terms are fair depends largely on whose arm is longer.

ASSET ALLOCATION, *n.* The art—and purported science—of choosing how much money to divide among which ASSET CLASSes. Assets with low CORRELATION tend to offer divergent patterns of risk and return, so an intelligent asset allocation consists of holdings that go up and down at different times and rates. You should welcome owning assets that lose money some of the time, because they are likely to end up making money when your other holdings go down.

Asset allocation accounts for the vast majority of the differences in results among investors, dwarfing other factors such as exactly which securities they buy, or when they buy or sell. However, instead of using math or logic to determine a recommended asset allocation, many financial advisors use guesswork or promote whatever has been hottest lately.

Almost no advisors recommended an allocation to gold in 1999, when the precious metal had lost money for two decades. By 2011, when gold had tripled over the previous five years, many put at least 10 percent of their clients' assets in it—right before it collapsed.

Similarly, a presentation to the prestigious Institute of Chartered Financial Analysts in 1986 recommended that a "conservative investor" with $100,000 allocate as much as 15 percent to limited partnerships. Why? Data full of BACKFILL bias and SURVIVORSHIP BIAS showed that real-estate partnerships had earned an average of 13.2 percent annually over the previous fifteen years, twice the return on stocks. Over the ensuing decade, however, most limited partnerships ceased to exist.

Whenever you consider a recommended asset allocation, ask which of the asset classes have *low* historical returns. If none of them do, you aren't being assigned an asset allocation. You're being invited to chase whatever is hot—most likely right before it's not.

ASSET CLASS, *n.* A category of investment offering its own distinctive risks and rewards, with low CORRELATION to other investments. Bonds, for instance, tend to do well when stocks do poorly, and vice versa. Commodities also tend to zig when stocks or bonds zag.

Not all asset classes are always worth owning, however, and not everything proclaimed to be an asset class is sufficiently distinctive to be one (*see HEDGE FUND*). If a "new" or "alternative" asset class costs a lot more to own than traditional categories like stocks and bonds, it probably won't turn out to have durable value.

ASSET GATHERING, *n.* How brokers, financial advisors, and portfolio managers describe what they do when no one else is listening. In plain English it means: "grabbing all the money we can with both hands from as many customers as possible so we can earn more fees for less work."

AUDITOR, *n.* In Latin, "one who hears"; in English, also one who obeys. All too often, accountants approve a company's financial statements exactly as the company's management wishes them to be presented.

> $ "It's our job as auditors to do whatever we can to ensure that a company's financial statements are presented fairly and accurately," said Seymour Billings, a partner in the Chicago office of the accounting firm of Tinker Hyde Alter & Berry, on a recent visit to one of his largest clients, a retail chain. "We're not policemen or fraud detectors," Mr. Billings added, while in the adjacent building, employees of the retailer loaded filing cabinets full of financial records into a garbage truck.

AVAILABILITY, *n.* A mental shortcut, or HEURIS-TIC, that leads people to judge the frequency or probability of events by how easily examples spring to mind. The vividness of rare events can make them seem more common and likely to recur than they are. Flying is among the safest ways to travel, but on the rare occasions when an airplane does crash, the fireball on the runway is broadcast worldwide and burned into the brain of everyone who sees it.

Market crashes are rare, too, but the spectacular damage they cause is also seared into the collective unconscious. That leads many investors to miss out on the gains stocks can generate during the surprisingly long periods between crashes.

The vast majority of initial public offerings (*see IPOs*) fail to outperform the market, but it takes only a few spectacular successes like Google to create the illusion that investing in IPOs is the road to riches. The vividness of huge gains on one stock makes such profits seem more probable than they are. *See also NEXT.*

AVERAGING DOWN, *v.* To buy a stock or other asset as its price keeps dropping—an action widely ridiculed, often by speculators who bought the same asset at twice the price and have already lost their shirts. However, assuming you have calculated a MARGIN OF SAFETY, you *should* be willing to buy more as the asset falls in price; it is, after all, getting cheaper.

AXE, *n.* The Wall Street analyst whose opinions hold the greatest sway over the price of a stock—until his or her hot streak runs out, at which point a new "axe" takes a whack at it. This bizarre cycle continues for decades without most investors ever noticing that the blade is never swung by the same person for long enough to be meaningful.

BACKFILL, *v*. To inflate the average return of HEDGE FUNDs by as much as 4 percentage points annually. Fund managers are not required to report their returns and may launch as many funds as they wish; thus, they can wait to see which fund turns out to do well before deciding whether to report its existence to the data services that calculate returns. The performance history of the INDEX that tracks the returns of hedge funds is then *backfilled* by the data service to include the performance of the fund back to its inception. The return of a fund that turns out to do poorly, meanwhile, may not get reported to the database at all. With good returns added back into the index over time and bad ones often excluded, the average performance of the index looks better, after the fact, than the returns of the hedge funds themselves were in real time.

If a CONSULTANT or FINANCIAL ADVISOR tells you that the average hedge fund in a particular category has earned an annual average of X percent, ask: "Is that number free of backfill bias?" If your advisor doesn't know what you're talking about, get a new one.

See also SURVIVORSHIP BIAS.

BACKTEST, *v.* and *n.* To comb through financial databases to determine which investing or trading techniques would have worked the best if anyone had known about them at the time. Many asset managers then use the backtests as a way to extract money from clients in the present— and disappoint them in the future.

Backtesting can be legitimate; just as you wouldn't buy a car without test-driving it or a house without going inside, you shouldn't manage your money without knowing how that investment approach performed in the past. All too often, however, backtesting is "overfitted," or designed to find any technique, no matter how obscure or absurd, that beat the market over some period, no matter how unusual the circumstances.

Imagine that you videotape people flipping a fair coin 1 million times. By luck alone, it's highly likely that one of them will flip heads ten times in a row. You scroll through thousands of hours of video until you find that sequence. You slow it down and study it, looking for something— anything—distinctive about how your tosser happened to be flipping during those particular moments.

As soon as you find your "CORRELATION," you can tell your clients that after studying 1 million coin flips, you have uncovered the secret to identifying tossers who can infallibly flip heads. You show them a video selection of flippers who produced disappointing, unclustered alternations of heads and tails. Then you triumphantly replay the video in the moments leading up to and including the ten heads in a row. "Look at his wrist," you say. "See how he twists it just before he flips the first one? *That's* what determines that he will get ten heads in a row."

People will pay you buckets of money for this.

But what you claim to have discovered in your backtesting is nothing but a statistical fluke. It is present in the *sample* (the frozen sequence you show your clients) but not in the *population* (the overall sequence of outcomes that will continue to unfold in the real world). You are counting on people to believe in REPRESENTATIVENESS, the cognitive illusion that a short-term sample of data predicts the results that are to be expected in the long term. The more vivid and surprising the short-term sample is, the more likely people are to believe that it will be replicated over the long run.

Whenever a financial advisor or money manager throws impressive "historical" numbers at you, ask: Are these results backtested? How far back did your data go? When did you begin running this strategy live, with real money? Have you made changes to it since, and if so, why? How many other strategies did you test before you settled on this one? (If the answer is greater than five, you should be suspicious.)

If you don't ask tough questions about performance that was plucked out of the past, you are likely to end up blindsided by the returns you get in the future.

BAIL OUT, *v.* Also: **BAILOUT,** *n.* What the managers of a bank do just before they run it into the ground; also, what the taxpayers are stuck doing to the bank afterward. As a result, the bank's top executives will individually be hundreds of millions of dollars richer, whereas the taxpayers will collectively be billions of dollars poorer.

As the influential journalist Ivana Neill recently recalled in her column, which chronicles the travails of powerful business figures:

💲 *"The critics of this company just don't get it," Xavier Butz, chief executive of Bailey Solvent, the giant investment bank in New York, told me during an interview in August 2008. "This firm will survive this crisis as we have all the others, and the very thought that we could ever need a bailout is absurd."*

When I reached him by phone a year later, the former CEO said adamantly, "We took that money only because the government forced it on us. We didn't want it, and we never needed it." He spoke loudly to be heard over the clanking of the ski lift at a resort in Argentina, where he was vacationing.

BALANCE SHEET, n. The part of a company's financial statements in which it reports its assets (what it owns) and its liabilities (what it owes). Total assets and total liabilities must "balance," or match. If they don't, the company's management or its accountants may put a finger or two on the scale until they do.

BANK HOLIDAY, n. A day on which banks are closed to celebrate national holidays or, if it happens to be early March 1933, a day on which banks are closed because they might go bust if they stayed open. Such emergency bank holidays will never occur again anywhere, of course.

A Run on the Bank by Depositors, photograph, 1933. FRANKLIN D. ROOSEVELT PRESIDENTIAL LIBRARY AND MUSEUM

....

Clay Model of a Sheep's Liver, Babylonian, ca. 1900–1600 BC.
TRUSTEES OF THE BRITISH MUSEUM

BARU, *n.* In ancient Mesopotamia, a priest who specialized in predicting the future by studying the contours of a liver or lung taken from a freshly sacrificed sheep.

The *baru* worked from an intricate template, often rendered as a clay map that charted dozens of variations on the surface of the sheep's organ, as in this example from the British Museum.

We may safely presume that when the *baru*'s predictions didn't come true, he blamed it on the dead sheep. The modern version of a Mesopotamian *baru* is known as a TECHNICAL ANALYST.

BASIS POINT, *n.* One-hundredth of 1 percent, or one ten-thousandth of the total, a proportion so puny-sounding that no one ever begrudges paying a few basis points of his or her wealth to a hardworking Wall Streeter. Multiply a few ten-thousandths across a few billion dollars, pounds, euros, or quatloos, however, and pretty soon you're talking real money. On $1 billion, for instance, 50 basis points equals $5 million.

💲 *"Our management fee is only 50 basis points," said Phil D. Hopper, a portfolio manager at the investment firm of Tucker, Cash & Left in Grosse Point, Michigan. "That's a bargain for the services we provide."*

*Asked why the license plate on his Maserati in the
firm's parking lot read "50 BPS," Mr. Hopper cleared his
throat and replied, "That stands for 50 bauds per second,
the speed of my first modem."*

BEAR, n. A speculator who makes a risky bet that the
price of an asset will go down—in opposition to a BULL
making a risky bet that it will go up.

The term appears to have originated in the London
stock market early in the eighteenth century. In the July 7,
1709, issue of his newspaper the *Tatler*, Sir Richard Steele
told this story: "A noble gentleman [and] major . . . bought
the 'bear' of another officer. . . . However, having sold the
'bear,' and words arising about the delivery, the most noble
major . . . abused the other with the titles of rogue, villain,
bearskin-man, and the like. . . . One who insures a real value
upon an imaginary thing, is said to sell a bear. . . ."

Note that at this early stage, *bear* was not the seller
but the asset being sold. The seller, whom we now would
call a bear or SHORT, was then called a *bearskin-man* or
bearskin-jobber.

That points back to an earlier English proverb, "to sell the
bear's skin before one has caught the bear," an apt description
of the transaction in which a speculator borrows and then sells
stock, betting that it can be bought back later at a lower price.

In the 1765 edition of the book *Every Man His Own
Broker* by the London barrister Thomas Mortimer, a bear
was a characterized as in

a continual hurry; always with alarm, surprize, and
eagerness painted on his countenance; greedily

swallowing the least report of bad news; rejoicing in
mischief, or any misfortune that may bring about the
wished-for change of [a fall in] the stocks, that he may
buy in low, and so settle his account to advantage . . .
with meagre, hagged [haggard] looks, and a voracious
fierceness in his countenance, [he] . . . seizes on all
who enter the Alley, and by his terrific weapons of
groundless fears,—and false rumours—frightens all
around him out of that property, he wants to buy.

Occasionally, bears seem like an endangered species, but
they are merely hibernating; at these moments, other investors should fear for their own survival.
See also SHORT.

BEAR MARKET, *n.* A phase of falling prices when
you can no longer bear to think about what a fool you were
for not selling your investments—which is generally a sign
that you should think instead about buying more. A period
of falling prices inevitably sets the stage for a period of rising
prices. *See also BULL MARKET.*

A bear market is commonly believed to begin when
a stock-market average or index has fallen by at least
20 percent. But, in fact, there is no official definition or
threshold—still another reminder that reality on Wall
Street is just a state of mind.

BEAT THE MARKET, *v.* To own or trade securities that perform better than a market average or
BENCHMARK—which, sooner or later, almost all securities will. However, they will tend either to stop beating the

market as soon as you buy them or to begin doing so as soon as you sell them. Thus, the investors who obsess the most over beating the market are the most likely to end up being beaten by it.

BEHAVIORAL ECONOMICS, *n.* The study of how human beings make decisions about money—as opposed to traditional or "standard" economics, which studies how ECONOMISTs think human beings would make decisions about money if all human beings thought the way economists think they do. BEHAVIORAL FINANCE is the subdiscipline that looks at how real people make decisions about investing.

"*Stocks Down,*"
Currier & Ives,
lithograph, ca. 1849.
LIBRARY OF CONGRESS

"*Stocks Up,*"
Currier & Ives,
lithograph, ca. 1849.
LIBRARY OF CONGRESS

$ "*Behavioral economics is nonsense,*" *said Maxim Eisen, a professor of economics at the University of Chicago. "People are rational: They know their preferences, efficiently process all information relevant to a financial decision, and calculate the expected value of any gamble based on the objective odds, not the emotions*

associated with it." His phone rang. "Hi, honey," he said,
then listened for a moment and screamed, "We won the
Powerball lottery?!"

BELLWETHER, *n.* A stock that sets the tone for the
rest of the companies in its industry; from the fourteenth-
century term for a sheep with a bell tied around its neck that
leads the flock. Like sheep following the leader, analysts and
investors scurry to change their opinions after an EARN-
INGS SURPRISE from a bellwether stock.

BENCHMARK, *n.* and *v.* An INDEX or basket of securities reflecting the average performance of a market, against
which the managers of a fund measure their return; the term
originates from the precise, standardized marks carved into
stone walls by surveyors to determine altitude throughout a
broad extent of land.

   When a fund consistently underperforms its benchmark,
the managers could fire themselves and put outsiders at the
helm, but that would be embarrassing. Instead, they either
begin CLOSET INDEXING or switch to a different benchmark that is easier to beat.

   See also CAREER RISK; RELATIVE PERFORMANCE.

BEST-IDEAS FUND, *n.* A mutual fund or hedge fund
that owns only the managers' favorite stocks—as opposed
to the other funds the managers run, which own dozens of
stocks they evidently don't like nearly as much. Although
there is some evidence that a handful of the best ideas
of portfolio managers will outperform the market, there
isn't much proof that funds of such best ideas are superior

investments. For an investor considering whether to buy a best-ideas fund, the best idea is to be skeptical.

BETA, *n.* The sensitivity of an investment's return to that of the market INDEX of which it is a component. A stock with a beta of 1.0, for instance, should return 10 percent if the index rises 10 percent and lose 10 percent if the market goes down 10 percent. At a beta of 1.5, the stock will gain 15 percent if the index goes up 10 percent and fall 15 percent on a 10 percent drop in the market; at a beta of 0.75, it will produce a 7.5 percent return in a 10 percent market; and so on. Traditionally, stocks with high betas have been regarded as offering higher risk and return; they have consistently delivered the former while perversely withholding the latter.

BIASED, *adj.* Human.

BIG BATH, *adj.* and *n. See KITCHEN-SINK.*

BIG FOUR, *n.* A shrinking number of accounting firms whose profits keep growing, something that cannot always be said of their clients—or of the people who invest in stocks or bonds issued by those clients on the basis of audits by the Big Four. Formerly known as the "Big Five," even earlier as the "Big Six," and before that as the "Big Eight," they now consist of Deloitte, Ernst & Young, KPMG, and PricewaterhouseCoopers. *See also AUDITOR; GAAP.*

BIG PRODUCER, *n.* A stockbroker or insurance agent who produces big commissions. The term is erroneous, however: The broker or agent doesn't produce the commissions. It is his clients who produce them. He just collects them.

BLOW-OFF, *n.* A sudden, steep rise in price accompanied by abnormally high trading; often believed to foretell a market drop. If the market goes up instead, the blow-off will be redesignated a "run-up," and the investors who were just told to stay away will now be urged to buy before the market leaves them completely behind. If enough of them buy fast enough, they will create a blow-off, thereby enabling the pundits who had warned of the blow-off to proclaim that they were right all along.

BLUE CHIP, *n.*; **BLUE-CHIP,** *adj.* The largest, most widely owned stocks, a term derived from casinos,

Enron Stock Certificate, 2002. MUSEUM OF AMERICAN FINANCE

where the most expensive chips are blue; a natural extension of the language of gambling to Wall Street, as speculators had long described buying stocks as "making a bet." Jargon can be prophetic: The label *blue chip* became popular about three years before the Crash of 1929. Once even the most conservative stocks were being described with a term minted in the casinos, a market crash could not be far away.

Among stocks regarded until recently as blue chips were Eastman Kodak, Enron, Nortel, Sears, Wachovia,

Washington Mutual, and WorldCom, all of which ended up going bust. Some blue chips stay royal blue; others turn their shareholders black and blue.

BLUE-SKY LAW, n. In the United States, a statute regulating the sale of securities within a particular state. The first blue-sky law was enacted in Kansas in 1911 after the state banking commissioner, Joseph Dolley, grew weary of watching his constituents get bilked by "fakers with worthless stock to sell." He nicknamed the law after charlatans who used to travel from farm to farm during a drought, collecting fees to spray a white liquid into the blue sky, claiming that it would bring rain—an activity not very different from peddling risky stocks to the unsuspecting.

BOARD OF DIRECTORS, n. A group of eminent businesspeople who set a corporation's policies and strategy. Boards of directors are often described as feckless collections of cronies, flunkies, lackeys, and patsies, but that view is unfair. Setting a corporation's policies and strategy requires exhaustive effort and research. That, in turn, necessitates playing an exhausting number of rounds of golf with the company's chief executive officer.

BOGEY, n. A source of fear or terror, related to *bogeyman*, an ancient reference to the Devil; now used to refer to an INDEX or BENCHMARK. That is appropriate, as many investment managers measuring their performance against a bogey are bedeviled by a chronic inability to beat the market.

§ *"Thanks to our skilled investment analysis and superior security selection, we beat our bogey this year by 10 percentage points, even more than our usual excess return," said senior portfolio manager Shirley M. Boggess of the investment-advisory firm Passmore Coyne & Co. of Beverly Hills, California. "We won't always outperform, of course—at least not by that much."*

BOILER ROOM, *n.* An operation staffed by brokers who use high-pressure sales pitches to steam money out of strangers over the telephone.

The origins of the term are variously explained by a belief that the practice originated in low-rent rooms next to the furnace in the basement of office towers, or by the observation that the arguments of the salesmen grow increasingly heated as they attempt to sweat money out of their prospective customers.

The movie *Boiler Room* understates the unpleasantness of such an operation, especially for the hapless investors who are its victims.

Detail from a Bestiary, British illuminated manuscript, fifteenth century.
THE ROYAL LIBRARY OF DENMARK

BONASUS, n. A mythical creature described by the ancient Romans and often included in medieval bestiaries, the bonasus closely resembles a bull, but with its horns curled back toward its tail. Because the horns are only for show, as the Roman naturalist Pliny wrote, the bonasus has no way to deter predators and will run away as soon as it is threatened. When it becomes panic-stricken, the bonasus spews immense quantities of flaming-hot manure in its wake. As the next stock-market crash will show, the typical investor who believes himself to be a BULL will turn out to be a bonasus. Do not stand too close behind him.

BOND, *n.* A contractual commitment made by a borrower to pay a debt back with INTEREST. Lenders who don't show enough interest in monitoring their investment, however, sometimes don't end up being paid back. A term probably of Teutonic origin, *bond* came to symbolize a pledge. Our modern expression "My word is my bond" is a direct descendant of an expression that appears in a version of the Lancelot legend, circa 1500: "O kingis word shuld be a kingis bonde." From this sense of strong obligation, it was a small leap to make a *bond* into a promise to repay a financial debt. Shylock, in Shakespeare's *The Merchant of Venice* (circa 1596), agreed to lend Antonio 3,000 ducats for three months if, in Shylock's words, Antonio would "go with me to a notary [and] seal me there your single bond." The word appears at least forty times in the play, as in Antonio's declaration:

> *Within these two months, that's a month before*
> *This bond expires, I do expect return*
> *Of thrice three times the value of this bond.*

Although Antonio wasn't thinking entirely of financial rewards, his remark makes it clear that bonds have long been associated with unrealistic expectations.

BONUS, *n.* On Wall Street, where success often goes as much to the lucky as to the skillful, bonuses are meant to motivate good performance but often backfire by inflaming the pursuit of risks that sensible people would otherwise avoid. The tradition of bonuses that can exceed 100 percent of salary dates back at least to 1902, when J.P. Morgan & Co. gave all its employees a full year's pay as a Christmas present after the firm launched the IPO of U.S. Steel that year. The word is derived from the Latin for *good,* which is precisely what a bonus is for its recipient, regardless of whether he or she did much to deserve it.

From a recent article by the financial journalist Heidi Story:

> $ *It's bonus season on Wall Street, and traders are expecting big payouts. "We've been on top of this market every quarter all year," said Juana Mercedes Furst, a proprietary trader at Bold, Braver & Riklis, the New York investment bank. "Nobody could beat the market four times in a row on luck alone, so we know the firm will take care of us at Christmastime this year." Trading profits are also on track to set a record at Sherwood Stoneham & Co., an investment bank in Piscataway, New Jersey. "Our models show that we haven't taken more risk, but we've taken smarter risk," said Anita Lamborghini, a proprietary trader there. "And our models have never been wrong yet."*

BOOK, *n.* The tally of positions, including profits and losses, held by a broker, trader, or money manager; reminiscent of the horse-racing term "to make book," or to place bets on the ponies for other people. The term dates back at least to Sir John Barnard's Act of 1734, a British law passed in the wake of the South Sea BUBBLE that sought to restrict speculative trading. One provision required every broker to keep "a Book or Register, known as the Broker's Book[,] in which he . . . shall enter all contracts."

REGULATORs ever since have been obsessed with inspecting brokers' "books and records," although such inspections rarely seem to catch any wrongdoing in time to protect investors.

As a verb, *to book* means to record or realize, as in "to book a profit" or "we booked a loss on that trade."

Brokers and financial advisors may also refer to their book of accounts, book of business, book of clients, book of customers, or book of production. These terms are all synonyms for *stream of fees*.

BOOK VALUE, n. Just as you should always know where the nearest exit is in an airplane, you should always check a company's book value: what remains after you subtract everything a company *owes* from everything it *owns*.

Book value is often derided as a poor measure of what companies are worth, because it imperfectly captures the potential value of patents, software, marketing innovations, and other "intangible" assets and fails to provide an accurate picture of a company's potential for generating cash. But it can be a rough guide as to what will be left for stockholders if something goes badly wrong.

BOTTOM, n. and v. As Thoreau wrote in *Walden*, "There is a solid bottom everywhere. We read that the traveller asked the boy if the swamp before him had a hard bottom. The boy replied that it had. But presently the traveller's horse sank in up to the girths, and he observed to the boy, 'I thought you said that this bog had a hard bottom.' 'So it has,' answered the latter, 'but you have not got half way to it yet.'" And investing is no different today. A market is said by TECHNICAL ANALYSTs to be "forming a bottom" when prices appear to be stabilizing after a period of falling. It is said to be "completing a bottom" when prices begin to rise. If prices then fall instead, technical analysts will simply declare that now the market is forming *another* bottom. New bottoms can be formed repeatedly—all the way down to zero, in fact. *See also SUPPORT.*

BOTTOM-UP, *adj.* Attempting to learn everything there is to know about a company's business; perhaps because such research is so difficult that only a few analysts and investors are intrepid enough to try it, the term is often garbled into *bottoms-up*. Although that may accurately describe the liquid or romantic activities that some analysts or investors engage in after work, *bottoms-up* should not be used to describe how these people do their day jobs. In the unlikely event that you ever encounter anyone who still does fundamental research, use the term *bottom-up* instead.

BOURSE, *n.* An exchange building or meeting place for traders, described in 1688 by a merchant in Amsterdam as the structure that encloses traders like a purse or the place where everyone seeks to fill his purse. "As the word 'purse' means skin in Greek, [so] it is that many players leave their skins." A synonym for STOCK EXCHANGE; borrowed from the French *bourse,* or "purse," from the Latin and Greek *bursa,* meaning "pouch" or "sac," originally a wineskin made out of hide. (For other financial terms whose early use was related to alcohol, *see BROKER; PANIC.*)

The Bourse of Bruges in the Fifteenth Century, engraving from Flandria Illustrata, 1641. GHENT UNIVERSITY LIBRARY

The financial use of the term is purported to have arisen in Bruges, Belgium. The aristocratic Van der Buerse or Van der Beurze family had run a hotel on the square since at least 1276. Its ancestral coat of arms, featuring three money bags or sacks (*bursae* in Latin), was carved onto the front of one of the family's buildings along the square. Trading occurred outdoors, under the sign of those *bursae,* thus leading the area to be called the "bursa."

Sharing the same root as "bursar" and "disburse," the word is also related to the medical terms *bursa* and *bursitis,* which can be caused by repetitive motion syndrome, a condition that can afflict frequent traders.

BREADTH, *n.* The stock market is said to have "bad breadth" when the number of falling stocks is greater than the number rising; although this financial halitosis is believed to predict further decline in the overall market, there is scant evidence that bad breadth indicates anything other than the obvious fact that a lot of stocks have been going down. Bad breadth tends to reek the worst right before a bull market begins. The market can also have good breadth when more stocks are rising than falling.

BREAKPOINT, *n.* The dollar amount at which investors in a mutual fund receive a discount on the commission they pay to the broker selling the fund. The breakpoint is typically set just below the breaking point, or the level at which the investors get disgusted with paying commissions entirely. Most funds with sales charges or LOADs have breakpoints; not all investors have a breaking point, although perhaps they should.

BRIGHT LINE, *adj.* and *n.* A line dividing ethical from unethical behavior that is often blurred until dull. The simplest "bright-line rule" or "bright-line test" answers the question: Would my mother be proud of me if she knew I was doing this? On Wall Street, the voice of Mom may be the least audible to those who most urgently need to listen to her. The financial industry would harbor much less darkness if every action had to pass Mom's bright-line test.

BROKER, *adj.* The comparative form of *broke*.

Also, used as a noun, a person who buys and sells stocks, bonds, mutual funds, and other assets for people who are under the delusion that the broker is doing something other than guesswork.

One early definition of a broker, sometimes attributed to the British lexicographer Samuel Johnson, is "a negotiator between two parties who contrives to cheat both."

The word *broker* derives from the Latin *brocca*, a spike or pointed instrument. In Middle English, as early as 1305, a *broche* was a lance or skewer. (The usage survives in a *brooch* that is fastened to clothing with a sharp pin.) Around 1377, William Langlois used it as a verb in *Piers Plowman*: "to broche hem with a pak-nedle [pack needle]."

By 1440, "to broche" meant to tap a barrel of wine or ale—a meaning related to our modern *broach the subject*, or to open a line of conversation. Soon, someone who retailed booze was known as a *brocheor, brokeor, brocour, brokour,* or *brogger.* The *brocheor* stood between the customer and the product, controlling the flow of liquid from the cask much as a modern broker taps the flow of capital. In an unsanitary age when alcohol was among the few liquids safe to drink, the *brocheor* performed a vital task and presumably was well paid.

Perhaps because the same cask or barrel can be tapped repeatedly, *brogger* came to describe an agent, someone who frequently releases or exchanges portions of a large quantity. By 1550, a royal proclamation declared that "no one shuld bie or sel the self-same thinges againe, except broggers."

Finally, in the late sixteenth century, the term extended to the financial markets; as one chronicler wrote in 1592: "There is an occupation of no long standing about London, called broking, or brogging, whether ye will; in which there is pretty jugling, especially to blind law, and bolster usury."

The roots of *brokerage* in dispensing alcohol were not entirely forgotten as the frenzied pursuit of wealth in the seventeenth and early eighteenth centuries reminded many observers of drunken debauchery. In *King John* (circa 1596), Shakespeare described Commodity, or economic self-interest, as "this bawd, this broker." *Broking* was even used as a mild

curse similar to *bloody* or *blasted*: In 1592, one author condemned someone for acting "like a broking varlet," and in
1606 another wrote, "I scorn that base, broking name."

The etymology of *broker* is unfamiliar to almost all
investors today, although its medieval roots in describing
someone who taps—and potentially drains—a source of
liquid wealth are well worth bearing in mind.

See also STOCKBROKER.

BUBBLE, *n.* A mania; a rise in asset prices that seems ir-
resistible at the time and irrational in retrospect; a bull market blown full of hot air until it reaches the bursting point.

The term is commonly believed to have originated
around 1719–1720, when shares in the Mississippi Co. in
France, the South Sea Co. in Britain, and the Dutch East
India Company in the Netherlands rose approximately tenfold in a matter of months and then collapsed.

But the word is older. To *bubble*, meaning to cheat or
trick, was a common term in England decades before the
Mississippi Co. mania. "Let them be bubbl'd by them that
know no better," wrote Daniel Defoe, in his pamphlet "The
Free-Holders Plea against Stock-Jobbing Elections of Parlia-
ment Men" (1701).

As a noun, "bubble" was also a synonym for someone
who had been robbed or defrauded. As the rake Dorimant
advises in George Etherege's Restoration comedy, *The Man
of Mode* (1676): "Lose it all like a frank gamester on the
square, 'twill then be time enough to turn rook [swindler]
and cheat it up again on a good substantial bubble."

The earliest joint-stock firms in England, which today
we would call publicly traded companies, date back to the

mid-sixteenth century; many were formed to exploit the newfound wealth of North America.

It seems feasible that a famous passage in Shakespeare's *Macbeth* (1607) was inspired by the early boom and bust in these joint-stock companies. In Act I, Scene 3, when the three witches, or "weird sisters," disappear before explaining their prophecies, Banquo cries, "The earth hath bubbles, as the water has, and these are of them. Whither are they vanish'd?" Macbeth answers, "Into the air, and what seem'd corporal melted as breath into the wind. Would that they had stay'd!"

Shakespeare, for whom words were always freighted with multiple meanings, could well have written this passage to draw painful laughs of recognition from the merchants in his audience. Many of these people had likely bought into the joint-stock bubbles that financed the American colonies— including the Virginia Co., which had set a tentative foothold in "Jamestowne" in 1606, just a few months before *Macbeth*'s debut.

The Dutch were also familiar with the word "bubble" (which they presumably borrowed from the English). It was closely related to *windhandel*, or "dealing in wind," the Dutch expression for trading in stocks that weren't in the speculator's possession, as SHORT-sellers may still do today. (*Windhandel* also referred to trading in derivatives such as options and futures.)

Joseph Penso de la Vega, who in 1688 wrote what is commonly regarded as the world's earliest book about the stock market, *Confusion de Confusiones,* described a stratagem used by short-sellers at the Amsterdam exchange: ". . . they offer for the stocks more than the price of the day (what we

*"Arlequyn Actionist," from Het Groote
Tafereel de Dwaasheid, Amsterdam,
1720.* THE LEWIS WALPOLE LIBRARY,
YALE UNIVERSITY

THE DEVIL'S FINANCIAL DICTIONARY   39

call 'inflating' the price). They influence the price this way in order to sell [short] at the higher figure and thus to gain in the end. God with one breath breathed life into Adam, whereas the bears take the life of many people by inflating the price [of the shares]. . . ."

This image—pumping up prices by puffing them full of air—may well be the origin of the financial term "bubble."

In de la Vega's image, a bubble literally brings stock prices to life. As a Spanish Jew who had considered becoming a rabbi, de la Vega would have known that the Hebrew word for "breath" or "wind," *ruach*, also means "spirit" or "soul." (The same was true in other ancient languages. In Greek, *pneuma* meant "soul," but also "breath" or "wind," a connotation that survives in English with such terms as "pneumatic drill" and "pneumonia." And, of course, to "animate," from the Latin *anima*, means to breathe life into someone or something.)

After several bubbles blew up and burst almost simultaneously, *windhandel* acquired a more scatological meaning. An explicit Dutch engraving from 1720, "Arlequyn Actionist," or "Harlequin the Stock Trader," shows securities dealers selling their offerings to a speculative mob through a unique distribution system: by breaking wind. Customers snatch stock certificates from the streams of gas blasting out of the brokers' posteriors—a fitting metaphor for investments that ended up too foul to touch.

This vulgar meaning of *windhandel* may already be foreshadowed in *Macbeth*, when the three sisters cackle, "I'll give thee a wind. . . . And I another."

From almost the birth of financial markets, people have understood that bubbles turn from invigorating to disastrous in the wink of an eye. In more recent times, "bubble" has been used indiscriminately by investors to describe any asset that they think is overpriced. Reliably identifying and steering clear of bubbles, however, has never been easy and probably never will be—except in hindsight.

See also HINDSIGHT BIAS.

BUCKET SHOP, *n.* A brokerage firm that defrauds investors through such high-pressure sales tactics as PUMP-AND-DUMP schemes; one level lower than a BOILER ROOM in the hierarchy of sleaze.

The term is said to have originated around 1820 in England, when street urchins rounded up beer kegs thrown away as empties by the pubs. The youths drank the dregs from the buckets and resold any remaining contents at cut-rate prices in abandoned storefronts that became known as "bucket shops." Or it may derive from nineteenth-century Chicago, where the Board of Trade required that transactions in wheat and other grains be for a minimum of 5,000 bushels, so traders who wanted lesser quantities had to buy "buckets" from speculators who broke up the minimum orders into smaller units.

In late nineteenth-century and early twentieth-century America, bucket shops operated as alternative stock and commodity markets, catering to individual speculators who were underserved by the major exchanges. Originating around 1877 after the spread of the telegraph and the TICKER, the bucket shops purchased private telegraph wires from Western Union and other providers, enabling them to display up-to-the-moment prices for stocks and commodities in their lavish offices.

Although the displayed prices were real, the transactions weren't. Bucket shops didn't place their customers' orders at any of the exchanges. Instead, customers borrowed on MARGIN from the bucket shop to make wagers on whether a stock or commodity would go up or down; all bets were against the house.

Even though it was all but impossible to win on stocks by betting at a bucket shop, the activity was enormously popular. In 1889, the *New York Times* estimated total daily trading volume at the nation's bucket shops at some 1 million shares, or more than four times the volume on the New York Stock Exchange.

A series of federal court cases and state laws finally stamped out traditional bucket shops around 1915, although the human urge to gamble against long odds or a rigged house has never been extinguished and probably never will be. Today's bucket shops, unlike those of old, place real trades for their customers—but the net result remains about the same.

BULL, *n.* A person who believes that an asset will go up in price, a belief often based exclusively on the fact that the person happens to own it. A bull in full stomp is almost incapable of absorbing any evidence suggesting that the asset might go down instead. *See CONFIRMATION BIAS.*

The term appears to have originated in contrast to *bear*. Charles Johnson's comic play *The Country Lasses* (1714) contains one of the earliest references: "Instead of changing honest staple for Gold and Silver, you deal in Bears and Bulls." In Colley Cibber's play *The Refusal* (1721), a character explains that all his wealth came from speculating in stocks: "Every shilling, Sir; all out of Stocks, Tuts, Bulls, Rams, Bears, and Bubbles." Note that *bulls* referred then to the stocks that buyers hoped to drive up in price, rather than to the buyers themselves.

In the popular imagination, the bull is the guardian of a placid herd of herbivores and is peaceful unless provoked, whereas the bear is more solitary and occasionally carnivorous. The bull tosses things up with his head and horns, whereas the bear tears fruit and honey down from trees with his sharp claws. These two stereotypes of animal behavior have come to symbolize the distinction between the contented herd of bullish buyers and the rampaging, destructive bearish sellers.

However, the terms were used in a more nuanced way in the eighteenth century. In the sixth edition of his book *Every Man His Own Broker,* published in London in 1765, barrister and speculator Thomas Mortimer wrote: "[The bull] goes lowering up and down around the house, and from office to office; and if he is asked a civil question, he answers with a surly look, and by his dejected gloomy aspect, and moroseness, he not badly represents the animal he is named after."

Note that Mortimer is directly contradicting the picturesque popular notion of a vigorous bull "tossing things up with his horns." In fact, Mortimer added, the bull was "sulky and heavy, and sits in some corner in a gloomly [*sic*] melancholy posture," unlike the BEAR, who had "a voracious fierceness in his countenance."

Although the American stock market didn't launch until the 1790s, the terminology caught on quickly. On January 31, 1805, US representative John Randolph of Virginia stood up in Congress to denounce the Yazoo land scam, in which speculators had sold land west of Georgia at obscene prices. Some victims wanted compensation from the federal government. "As well may your buyers and sellers of stock, your bulls and bears of the alley, require indemnification for their losses at the hands of the nation," thundered Randolph.

By the 1830s the terms *bull* and *bear* were common, and by the 1840s they were used as both nouns and verbs. "To bull" a stock was the orchestrated effort by speculators to manipulate the price upward.

Frederick Jackson, in *A Week in Wall Street by One Who Knows* (1841), wittily summed up the two main species in the market: "a Bear means a man who has no shares in the Stocks—one stripped—in an em-bar-assed condition . . . a Bull means a man who has more shares than he can keep, and has gored his neighbor to procure them."

By 1879, bulls and bears so thoroughly personified Wall Street speculation that the artist William Holbrook Beard populated paintings entirely with them.

BULL MARKET, *n*. A period of rising prices that leads many investors to believe that their IQ has risen at least as much as the market value of their portfolios. After the inevitable fall in prices, they will learn that both increases were temporary. *See BEAR MARKET.*

BUTTON UP, *v*. To hide investment losses from other people—and from oneself.

The term dates back at least to 1841, when Wall Street chronicler Frederick Jackson wrote: ". . . the stock went down, down, down, and not a purchaser could be found at any price . . . and strange as it may seem, not a man could be found in Wall-street, who confessed the ownership of a share; where three weeks before there were thousands. This is called buttoning up."

Forever gazing into a rearview mirror made of rose-colored glass, most investors pretend that their losses never happened. That makes them feel better about the past but also makes a realistic view of the future almost impossible.

BUY, *v.* What Wall Street analysts say investors should almost always do, regardless of a stock's price or market conditions. *See also SELL.*

BUY-AND-HOLD, *v.* and *adj.* To hang on for the long term in an asset like stocks—thus infuriating most market "experts," who advise frequent trading in and out in response to actual or imaginary risks and opportunities. At its best, buy-and-hold investing is stupefyingly boring. At its worst, during BEAR MARKETs, it feels like a failure. Therefore, critics are constantly declaring that "buy-and-hold is dead." They never offer persuasive evidence, however, that any alternative has worked better over the long term. If buy-and-hold is dead, what is alive?

BUYBACK, *n.* The repurchase of a portion of its outstanding STOCK by the company that issued it—typically carried out most enthusiastically when the company's shares are most overvalued, and often abandoned when they are at their cheapest. Anyone who thinks "Buy high, sell low" describes only the Wrong-Way Corrigan behavior of individual investors doesn't know much about how corporations allocate their own capital.

BUY THE DIPS, *v. See DIP.*

CALL, *adj.*, *n.*, and *v.* A term for several Wall Street practices that will soon lead you to call yourself a fool if you don't know what you are doing: (1) a *call loan* is made by a brokerage to its customers trading on MARGIN on condition that the firm may demand, or "call," the money back at any time; (2) a *call auction* at a STOCK EXCHANGE aggregates all bids and offers for a security until as many of the trades as possible are matched; (3) a *call OPTION* confers the right to buy a security at a certain price on or before a specific date; (4) a *bond call* enables a company or government to pay off a borrowing prematurely, typically at the worst imaginable time for its investors.

CAPITAL, *n.* The wealth of an individual, company, or nation, a word deriving from the Latin *caput*, or head—paradoxically, the organ that many investors use the least in their effort to amass capital.

Capitalism is, therefore, the art of using one's head. But it also invokes the animal nature of wealth. In many cultures, livestock was the safest store of value. Cattle, sheep, and goats transform common grass into a steady supply of protein

in the form of meat and milk—much the way capital, properly tended, can be a reliable source of investment income.
Capital may have come to describe wealth because so many
preindustrial societies measured prosperity by the quantity
of livestock a family owned, counting it as so many "head of
cattle." The more head of livestock a family had, the more
capital it had.

In the ancient Middle East, as in rural areas of the world
today, livestock was the most prestigious measure of prosperity. In the Book of Genesis, when Cain offers God an offering of "the fruit of the ground," the Lord rejects it in favor
of Abel's sacrifices of "the firstlings of his flock." Putting first
things first, Genesis 13:2 describes Abraham as "very rich in
cattle, in silver, and in gold."

We tend to think of capital as quasi-permanent, but we
would all be better off if we kept the origins of the word
in mind: like the livestock it is named for, capital is prone
to wander, stampede, and even perish if not carefully
shepherded.

CAPITAL STRUCTURE, *n. See STACK.*

CAPITULATION, *n.* The act of giving up on a falling
financial market by selling out one's position, named after
the ancient practice of removing one's cap as a gesture of
surrender to a superior opponent. In severe market declines,
Wall Street pundits will declare that they are waiting for
"signs of capitulation," typically described as massive waves
of selling at distressed prices. However, BEAR MARKETs
tend to end not with a bang but with a whimper; they dwindle away into a dark stupor. BULL MARKETs begin not

when panicked investors capitulate, but when grim and hopeless investors become too paralyzed even to sell.

CAREER RISK, n. The risk that, by thinking independently, a money manager might lose clients, endanger a big salary, and harm his or her career; for money managers, the only risk that matters. When professional investors are right, no one will ask why; their clients will be too busy counting their profits to seek an explanation. But when money managers are wrong, their clients will immediately want to know why they made the mistake. Portfolio managers can either be wrong in a crowd, in which case no one will blame them for making the same mistake everybody else made, or "wrong and alone," in which case they will look like idiots.

The only way to outperform the market average is to do something different. Although that may work over the long run, it is all but certain to produce disappointing results at least some of the time in the short run—making the manager appear wrong and alone.

Because of career risk, it is rational for money managers to do irrational things, such as buying stocks that are already overpriced, selling undervalued stocks before they have time to grow to their full potential, and measuring a portfolio's performance relative to the market over periods as short as a single day to make sure the results don't deviate too far from it.

Together, these actions lead to excessive trading and an obsessive focus on imitating whatever the market is doing, rather than on figuring out what the manager should be doing: selecting the cheapest stocks and holding them for years at a time. Whenever you hear fund managers talk about how important "risk management" is to them, make sure you understand whose risk they are primarily seeking to manage: their own.

CARRIED INTEREST, *n.* A tax dodge that allows the billionaires and centimillionaires who run PRIVATE-EQUITY FUNDs to pay taxes on much of their earnings at lower rates than many members of the middle class. These folks generally earn fees equal to 20 percent of profits on the funds' assets. For tax purposes, that income is characterized as "carried interest," a long-term investment that produces a capital gain or loss taxed at a maximum of 23.8 percent. Most other prosperous people in the United States pay taxes on income at rates that can exceed 43 percent.

Off the record, many executives in the private-equity industry admit that carried interest is a preposterously unfair giveaway that should be abolished. Officially, however, they defend it as a fair and rational incentive that encourages long-term investment. If you could earn hundreds of millions of dollars per year and pay tax on much of it as if you had earned only a couple hundred thousand dollars, wouldn't you feel the same way?

Those who mistake wealth for logic often defend the tax treatment of carried interest as if it made sense. As the financial journalist Ivana Neill recently wrote in a column entitled "Give Private Equity a Break":

> $ *"There's no evidence justifying the view that carried interest is unfair or that it contributes to income inequality,"*

said Claire Lee Craven, an analyst at Lord, King,
Prince, Baron, Duke, Earl, Noble, Squires & Masters,
a consulting firm to the private-equity industry. Also last
week, I reached Maximilian Bucks, chief executive of the
private-equity firm Moore, Moore & Moore. "It's anti-
American to tax carried interest as ordinary income," he
said. "Carried interest is an investment in the future!"
Mr. Bucks added, "And that stuff about paying tax at the
same rate as my secretary is ridiculous. I even do my own
mail." As if to prove it, Mr. Bucks was stuffing checks
into envelopes that he had hand-addressed to members of
Congress.

CATOBLEPAS, n. The modern financial form of a mythical beast resembling a bull, but with a head so heavy that it
is incapable of looking up. Ancient and medieval bestiaries
describe the catoblepas as having poisonous breath and a
thick mane that always
covers its eyes. The con-
temporary catoblepas is
the investor who says he
will put money to work—
just not today, because
the economy is terrible
and UNCERTAINTY is

too high. Tomorrow, he
will again say he will put
money to work—just not
yet. He will continue to

Catoblepas, engraving from
Jan Jonston, Historiae
Naturalis de Quadrupedibus,
1657. ARCHIVE.ORG

look down and to hang his head. The higher the market
goes, the more vehemently the catoblepas will insist he is

really a BULL, the darker the view of his world will turn, and the more miserable he will become.

CENTRAL BANK, *n.* A group of economists who believe that their current forecasts will turn out to be accurate even though their past forecasts have been unreliable, that their present policies will succeed even though their past policies have failed, that they can prevent inflation from occurring next time even though they didn't prevent it last time, that they can foster lower unemployment in the future even though their practices worsened it in the past, and so forth.

You now should be able to answer this riddle: What's the difference between a central banker and a weathervane? They both turn in the wind, but only the central banker thinks he or she determines which way the wind blows.

CERTAINTY, *n.* An imaginary state of clarity and predictability in economic and geopolitical affairs that all investors say is indispensable—even though it doesn't exist, never has, and never will.

The most fundamental attribute of financial markets is *uncertainty.* Just when you think you know what is sure to happen, the financial markets are about to prove that you are wrong.

Whenever turmoil or turbulence becomes obvious, pundits proclaim that "investors hate uncertainty." But UNCERTAINTY is the only condition investors ever have faced, or ever will, from the moment barley and sesame first began trading in ancient Mesopotamia to the last trade that will ever take place on Planet Earth.

The unexpected will always occur—over and over again, until the end of time. And pundits will forever try to predict what will happen next. But if anyone could predict it, then it wouldn't be unexpected. Thus, hating uncertainty is a waste of time and energy. You might as well hate gravity or protest against the passage of time. The only certainty is that uncertainty will never go away. Get used to it, or get out of the markets entirely and stay out.

CETERIS PARIBUS, *adj. phr.* "All else being equal" or "all other things held constant." A phrase used by ECON-OMISTs to refer to a set of circumstances that anyone else would describe with the word "never."

> $ *"If you earn a sum of money working and the same sum from playing the lottery, you will spend them in the same way,* ceteris paribus," *said Ivy Tower, a professor of economics at Harvard University, on a recent walk across campus. A $100 bill blew across the path, and she speared it with the stiletto of her right shoe. "Now I can buy the new Kindle," she said triumphantly.*

CHANNEL CHECK, *n.* A phase of Wall Street research in which an analyst purports to visit warehouses, stores, and other physical locations to verify that a company's goods and prices match its reports. If the reliability of channel checks is any guide, analysts appear to conduct them in the den of their own homes, checking that the channel they are watching on TV is the same as the one on the remote control they are holding.

CHECKLIST, n. A tool leading to such methodical decisions that it is rarely used by most investors, who have much more fun—but make much less money—relying instead on snap judgments based on intuition and emotion. The structure provided by a good checklist forces investors to do careful and original research, combats CONFIRMATION BIAS by seeking out information that challenges their own views, and accounts for REGRESSION TO THE MEAN by requiring multiple sources of data over the long term. Like the checklists employed by airline pilots and emergency medical workers, which can save lives, a good investing checklist prevents impulsive decision making. No wonder so few investors use one.

CHINESE WALL, n. You might think that this barrier, intended to minimize any CONFLICT OF INTEREST within a Wall Street firm, would have to be a mighty fortification made of stone and brick and compressed earth like the Great Wall of China, after which it is named; instead, it is a few sheets of paper written by the firm's own lawyers. The Great Wall of China kept invaders out; Chinese walls seem to be effective at keeping conflicts *in*.

CHURCH, n. A place where the faithful worship God; also sometimes a place that the greedy use as a pretext for separating the faithful from their money, as when fraudsters run PONZI schemes or other forms of AFFINITY FRAUD. Every year, hundreds of millions of dollars are stolen in predatory investment schemes by con artists who exploit other people's faith in God. Churchgoers should remember the exhortation of Jesus in the Book of Matthew: "No man can serve two masters: for either he will hate the one, and love the other; or else he will hold to the one, and despise the other. Ye cannot serve God and mammon."

Disgraceful numbers of people are willing to prey upon those who pray. Believers should always bear in mind that faith in God does not justify credulity in financial schemes.

CHURN, *v.* To trade a portfolio so rapidly that the only positive returns are earned by the brokerage firm that fills the orders. Formerly committed almost exclusively by stockbrokers, churning has become a common form of financial hara-kiri, in which specu-lators who mistakenly call themselves "investors" rapidly trade their portfo-lios over and over again. So long as any money remains in their accounts, they refer to what they are doing as "learning how to trade." When their balances hit zero, their education will be complete.

Woman Churning Butter, J. W. Dunn, photograph, ca. 1897. Library of Congress

CIGAR BUTT, *n.* A stock bought so cheaply that it should go up even if the underlying business struggles to produce any cash.

As Warren Buffett put it: "If you buy a stock at a suffi-ciently low price, there will usually be some hiccup in the fortunes of the business that gives you a chance to unload at a decent profit, even though the long-term performance of the business may be terrible. . . . A cigar butt found on the street that has only one puff left in it may not offer much of a smoke, but the 'bargain purchase' will make that puff all profit."

Cigar butts have become even harder to find in financial markets than in the gutters of cities with anti-tobacco campaigns. And it takes a lot of butts at one puff apiece to form a PORTFOLIO.

CLEARLY, *adv.* Unclearly.

Analysts and pundits using the word "clearly" are either (1) pretending, without any valid evidence, that they know what is going to happen, or (2) describing what has already happened and declaring, after the fact, that they knew it would happen when at the time they had no idea (*see HINDSIGHT BIAS*).

CLIENTS, *n.* Also known, on Wall Street, as *muppets, flunkies, chumps, suckers, marks, targets, victims* or *"vics," dupes, baby seals, sheep, lambs, guppies, geese, pigeons,* and *ducks* (as in "When the ducks quack, feed 'em").

Although many investors were outraged by the revelation, in 2012, that some employees of Goldman Sachs called their clients "muppets," comparing customers to stuffed animals in a children's television show is quite flattering by historical standards. In his "The Anatomy of Exchange-Alley" (1719), Daniel Defoe referred to the typical investor as a "gudgeon," or someone as stupid as a fish, and a "cull," or simpleton.

Brokers and investment bankers have long been regarded (often by themselves) as predators. In "An Essay on the South Sea Trade," published in London in 1712, Defoe called

stockbrokers "Man-eating Discounters . . . those *Cannibals*."
The essayist Richard Steele, in the *Tatler* of May 25, 1710,
used "beast of prey" as a synonym for "trader." Although
the relationship between stockbrokers or financial advisors
and their clients has improved enough for the term *client* to
sound plausible, it is still far from fair and equal.

CLOSET INDEXING, *n*. The most inactive form
of ACTIVE investing, in which a PORTFOLIO MAN-
AGER chooses to own almost exactly the same securities
as an INDEX FUND, thus minimizing the odds of badly
underperforming it while maximizing his or her fees. *See also
CAREER RISK; RELATIVE PERFORMANCE.*

COMMISSION, *n*. The unit of currency on Wall Street,
always set at a level designed to maximize the trading volume generated by speculators swept up in the frantic attempt
to make the treadmill they are running on go even faster.
People who trade rapidly with no regard to commissions evidently believe that you can somehow outrace a treadmill by
increasing its velocity. Commissions can be as high as 10–15
percent of the amount invested and as low as 0.1 percent or
less; the more often you pay them, the richer your broker gets.
   The tale is still told of Country Cousin who visits Man-
hattan for the first time in the 1890s. Staring up at the tall
buildings on Wall Street, where City Cousin works, Country
Cousin exclaims, "Who built these amazing towers?" City
Cousin replies simply: "Customers did."

COMMODITIES, *n*. Assets that can be extracted,
drilled, harvested, melted, hammered, stretched, burned,

boiled, baked, pounded, fried, or eaten; so can the people who think they are investing in them.

Since at least the fifteenth century, *commodity* has meant something measurably advantageous, or a substance useful when it is changed from one form to another, from the Latin *com* (together) and *modus* (measure). Until the early nineteenth century, it was also sometimes used as a synonym for greed; although most dictionaries regard that meaning as archaic, it lives on in the financial markets.

Commodities have been traded for approximately 4,000 years; much of the Code of Hammurabi, in ancient Mesopotamia, was devoted to regulating the futures-trading market. Babylonian priests used astrological and occult signs,

including "patterns" they purported to detect in the livers and other organs of sacrificial animals, to predict prices in the futures markets for barley, silver, and other commodities. *See BARU.*

Commodities Being Traded in Amsterdam, Boëtius Bolswert, etching, 1609. RIJKSMUSEUM

Even in 1700 BC, commodities traded largely as futures, or standard contracts to buy or sell a fixed quantity of a product at an agreed price, to be delivered on a given date in the future. Speculators in ancient times probably financed such trading with borrowed money, as they do today.

There are three main ways to make or lose money on commodities. First, the market, or "spot," price can go up or down. Second, you earn a positive "roll return" if you can sell this month's futures contract for more than it costs you to buy next month's. Finally, you earn interest on the collateral that secures the borrowed money that you have riding on your bet.

Historically, the roll return has accounted for about half the long-term performance of commodities, but it has waned recently as a rush of money from Johnny-come-lately speculators distorted prices in the market for futures. And collateral return, which was substantial when interest rates averaged 5 percent or higher, has dwindled since the financial crisis of 2008–2009, with central banks squashing interest rates toward zero.

Thus, many of the naïve traders who stampeded into commodities were pursuing sources of return that had disappeared.

Unlike bonds, stocks, and real estate, commodities generate no predictable cash flows. So when their value depends entirely on what someone else will pay for them, they are even more dangerously exposed to the whims of the market than bonds, stocks, and real estate. No wonder commodities are called "alternative investments" by those who sell them to those who don't understand them.

COMPLIANCE, n. The set of procedures by which a financial firm obligates its employees to observe the letter of the law while freeing them to violate its spirit. Employment at compliance departments is booming on Wall Street. The spirit of the law, meanwhile, is enforced by the conscience department—which is perennially understaffed. As Warren Buffett has noted, "Lately, those who have traveled the high road in Wall Street have not encountered heavy traffic."

CONCENTRATION, CONCENTRATED FUND,
n. See BEST-IDEAS FUND.

CONFIDENCE, *n.* A quality, similar to religious belief but grounded on much shakier evidence, that tends to
be high when it should be low and low when it should be
high. Periods of high confidence are pernicious; the better
investors feel now, the more likely they are to be sorry later.
Almost no one can acknowledge that at the time, however.
See HINDSIGHT BIAS; OVERCONFIDENCE.

CONFIRMATION BIAS, *n.* The tendency of the
human mind to seek and favor evidence supporting a preexisting belief and to discount, ignore, or reject information
undermining that belief. As the poet Ogden Nash wrote, a
mind that is already made up is like a door that can only
open outward, so "the only result of the pressure of facts
upon it is to close it more snugly."

Confirmation bias is so universal and insidious that investors must force themselves, through such procedures as
CHECKLISTs, to seek out and consider evidence indicating
that their judgments could be wrong. Otherwise, investors
will remain trapped in the echo chambers of their own
minds, which ring forever with the words *I am right, and
everyone else is wrong.*

You are probably telling yourself as you read this that you
do not suffer from confirmation bias. Could your certainty
be evidence that, in fact, you do?

CONFLICT OF INTEREST, *n.* A preposterously
unlikely scenario in which the employee of a financial firm

who could earn ungodly amounts of money by acting against a client's best interest might proceed to do exactly that. Conflicts of interest are pervasive, if not universal, on Wall Street. They are not a problem, according to Wall Street, because financial firms do something better than eliminating them: "managing" them. *See also CHINESE WALL; DISCLOSURE; POTENTIAL CONFLICT OF INTEREST.*

CONSENSUS, n. The mean estimate among Wall Street ANALYSTs of what a company will earn next quarter, expressed in pennies per share. It is called a "mean" estimate not because it is cruel but rather because it is a statistical average. Anyone who believes that the mean estimate is accurate to the penny, however, is the victim of a cruel joke.

CONSULTANT, n. In the money-management business, an expert who charges high fees for advising clients to put their money into hot investment strategies that are about to go cold. In order to generate the needed cash, the consultant advises the clients to withdraw their money from cold investment strategies that are about to get hot. The clients willingly assent to such advice year after year because it gives them someone other than themselves to blame for the abysmal results.

CONTAGION, n. A condition in which raw emotions, particularly fear, spread epidemically from one investor to another, one market to another, and even around the world. There are only three known cures: time, quarantine, or ear plugs.

CONTRARIAN, *n.* A sheep masquerading as a lone wolf.

To be a contrarian, you must buy when most others are selling and sell when most are buying—an act that sounds easy but requires almost superhuman emotional toughness. Most money managers would destroy their businesses if they thought independently, as the typical client just wants them to chase whatever is hot until it is not.

When markets fall apart, investors who call themselves contrarians turn out to be conformists. Much like the Judean crowd chanting "We are all individuals!" in Monty Python's *Life of Brian*, all professional investors say they are contrarians. Almost none are.

See also CAREER RISK; HERDING.

CONVICTION, *n.* An intense belief, approaching certainty, that an asset will go up or down in price. A *high-conviction idea* is one that an investor is nearly 100 percent positive about—and is thus even more likely than usual to be wrong about. *See also OVERCONFIDENCE.*

CORE, *adj.* Central and indispensable to an investment strategy, at least for now.

CORE AND EXPLORE, *adj.* and *n.* Jargon used to describe a strategy that is faulty in theory but lucrative in practice for financial advisors: holding INDEX FUNDs for large US stocks and using ACTIVE management for everything else, on the false premise that active management is more effective in other ASSET CLASSes. Because of the ever-present chance that active managers might take reckless risks, the strategy might more accurately be called "core and explode."

CORE HOLDING, *n.* Any security that a professional fund manager has held for more than a year, give or take a few months; also, a holding that he or she is about to sell in a panic.

CORPORATE GOVERNANCE, *n.* The process by which companies are run for the benefit of their managers and a few powerful outside owners while claiming to treat every investor equally. Companies that boast of their "strong corporate governance" protect a fortunate handful of investors unusually well and everyone else equally badly.

CORRECTION, *n.* A moderate decline in the market that the people who think they have recognized it believe will not last much longer. It could, however, turn out to be the beginning of a full-blown BEAR MARKET, nothing but a DIP, or the beginning of a BULL MARKET. Only after it is over will anyone know for certain what it was.

The commonly used meaning is a decline of no more than 10 percent, although there is no official definition of a correction. Investors should note the connotation implicit in the term: that something about the market's behavior needed to be "corrected," as if it were somehow inherently wrong for prices to be rising.

CORRELATION, *n.* The extent to which securities or financial assets tend to move in tandem. Those who flatter themselves on being brilliant enough to buy assets that all go up at once should remember that, sooner or later, these highly correlated assets may all go down at once, too. If one asset has an above-average—or below-average—return and so does the other, they are said to be "positively" or highly correlated. If one has a higher return while the other is lower and vice versa, they are "negatively" correlated. If a higher return on one is associated with either a higher, lower, or average return on the other, then they are uncorrelated. DIVERSIFYing is most efficient and powerful when assets in a PORTFOLIO are not highly correlated. However, because that always requires owning some assets that will underperform others—rather than chasing whatever is hot at the moment—it will forever be unattractive to most investors. *See also STOCK-PICKERS' MARKET.*

COUNTERPARTY, *n.* The person or firm on the other side of the trade from you—the buyer if you are selling or the seller if you are buying. Fewer trades might be initiated if more investors visualized the counterparty climbing up onto the counter and partying, which often is exactly what happens when trading orders come in.

COUPON, *n.* The interest that the issuer of a bond promises, by contract, to pay to the holders of the debt. The term originates from the Old French *coupon,* or "piece cut off," from *couper,* "to cut," based on the traditional practice of snipping a certificate of interest from a bond and presenting it for payment. *See INDENTURE. Couper,* in French, also means "to deliver a blow," a meaning familiar to anyone who owns a bond whose issuer has skipped paying a coupon.

COVENANT, *n.* A detail in the contract, echoing the human rite of circumcision, that circumscribes the rights of a borrower and governs the terms under which a bond is issued. *See BOND; INDENTURE.*

As early as 1385 or so, when Geoffrey Chaucer wrote *The Legend of Good Women,* the word *covenant* was already common to describe a pledge of honor: "And in myn self this couenaunt made I." The word soon took the narrower meaning, which it retains today, of the specific promises enumerated in a financial contract: In Shakespeare's *Cymbeline* (1610), Posthumus Leonatus pledges a diamond ring as security for a bet, saying, "Let there be covenants drawn between us."

In *The Merchant of Venice,* Shylock stipulates that if Antonio can't repay a 3,000-ducat, three-month bond with cash, then Shylock is entitled to carve off "an equal pound of your fair flesh." Shakespeare, who treated every word as a mine of meaning, probably invoked the image of a pound of flesh as an allusion to the covenant between Abraham and God, in which the Lord commanded Abraham to "be circumcised in the flesh of your foreskin."

Borrowers and lenders alike would be better off if they bore in mind the ancient origins of the word *covenant* in the biblical ritual that symbolized the bond of honor between man and God.

COVER, *v.* To buy back a SHORT at a loss, in an attempt to eliminate the chance of further loss. Also, to follow a stock, as in "the analyst covers IBM." Also, the extent to which a borrower's generation of cash exceeds the interest on its debt, as in "Schlimazel Corp. has 1.2 times cover."

In the United Kingdom, a synonym for MARGIN. Each sense of the word potentially illuminates a different form of futility.

CRASH, *v.* and *n.* To collapse or drop in price by a frightening amount; a broad and sudden decline that sweeps through a financial market. An onomatopoeic, or imitative, word that mimics the sound of something shattering, *crash* dates back in English to about 1400. (*Craze*, which takes its meaning from the supposedly distinctive fissures in a lunatic's skull, likely shares the same root.)

"Crowd of People Gather Outside the NYSE Following the Crash of 1929," photograph, 1929.
Library of Congress

Surprisingly, *crash* wasn't a familiar financial term as late as 1817, when the poet Samuel Taylor Coleridge described the typical credit collapse, in his *Biographia Literaria*, as "a rapid series of explosions (in mercantile language, a crash), and a consequent precipitation of the general system."

When William Armstrong published *Stocks and Stock-Jobbing in Wall-Street* in 1848, he used the word repeatedly. However, at least in the United States, it then usually meant a sudden fall in a single stock, not in the entire market. A general drop in the stock market in Armstrong's day was an "explosion," a "break," a "crisis," or a "convulsion."

Until recent decades, "crash" was applied to describe catastrophic declines like that of the Great Depression, when the US stock market lost 84 percent between September 1929 and July 1932. More recently, it has been used by the financial media to describe such events as the Dow Jones Industrial Average declining from, say, 17,246 to 16,933 in a single day—the equivalent, in percentage terms, of a drop in temperature on a single day all the way from a balmy 68° F to a frigid 66.8° F. Brrrrrrrrr!!!

CREDIT, *n*. From the Latin for "faith" or "belief"; a loan, usually to a corporation, from a lender or CREDITOR whose faith or belief in the borrower had better be founded on research rather than on hope and prayer.

CREDIT CARD, *n*. A thin slab of plastic that enables a person to feel pleasure today by incurring pain tomorrow.

CREDIT RATING, *n.* A series of letters denoting the purported quality of bonds or other securities, according to a RATING AGENCY such as Standard & Poor's, Moody's, or Fitch. Ratings generally range from the highest, AAA, to D for DEFAULT. Any bond rated AAA has nowhere to go but down; those rated D have nowhere to go but up. Further inferences from credit ratings may be regarded as speculative.

CREDITOR, *n.* From the Latin for "believer"; someone who lent money to a borrower and believes the loan will be repaid in full. That belief turns out to be true—most of the time.

CREDITORS' COMMITTEE, *n.* A group of believers who assumed they ran no risk in lending money to a borrower and who are now negotiating, under the auspices of a bankruptcy judge, to get some of it back.

CROWN-JEWEL DEFENSE, *n.* A technique a company uses to fend off a hostile TENDER OFFER, in which it sells off its most desirable businesses in order to make itself less desirable and thereby more likely to remain independent. In the choice between keeping their jobs or the company's most profitable assets, the company's managers choose their jobs. The shareholders might have other priorities, but no one asks for their opinion.

CURRENCY, *n.* A nation's money, from the Latin *currere,* to run or to flow. Once confidence in a nation's economy weakens, the populace may rush to convert local

*"The Battle About Money," Pieter van
der Heyden after Pieter Bruegel the Elder,
engraving, ca. 1570–1600.* LIBRARY OF CONGRESS

money to foreign currency, thereby further weakening the
value of local money and potentially resulting in a run on
the currency, which is both linguistically redundant and
economically frightening. The US dollar has avoided that
fate—so far.

CUSTOMERS' YACHTS, *n.* The nonexistent luxury
craft purchased by investors with the imaginary profits they
would have earned if any of the financial advice they got
was any good.

The expression "Where are the customers' yachts?"—the
title of Fred Schwed Jr.'s classic book, published in 1940—
is another way of saying "Why are you so rich while your

clients aren't?" It originated in a quip uttered by the witty short-seller William Travers, probably in the 1870s. The story was recounted in 1888 by Wall Street banker Henry Clews, who noted that Travers suffered from a severe stutter:

> As soon as it became known to the yachtsmen [in Newport, Rhode Island] that the renowned Travers had appeared on the deck of his yacht, a committee was assigned to convey to him the respects of the members of the squadron. When they came along-side his craft he invited them on board, and saw at a glance that they nearly all happened to be bankers and brokers. Casting his eyes across the glittering water, he beheld a number of beautiful white-winged yachts in the distance, and finding, by inquiry, that they all belonged to Wall Street well known brokers, he appeared thereby to be thrown momentarily into a deep reverie, and, without turning his gaze from the handsome squadron, finally asked his distinguished visitors, "Wh-wh-where are the cu-cu-customers' yachts?"

CYCLICAL, *adj*. Temporary (or believed to be), as in "this is a cyclical bull market" or "the rise in interest rates is cyclical."

Cyclical stocks are those whose goods or services are dis-cretionary; these companies suffer when customers buy less during recessions and prosper when consumers buy more during economic recoveries. Among the companies regarded as cyclical are hotel operators, auto manufacturers, and pro-ducers of construction equipment.

Danger can arise when investors come to assume that any trend or state is no longer cyclical but has rather become SECULAR or even permanent. It is then most likely to reverse through REGRESSION TO THE MEAN. As the financial writer James Grant has observed, "In markets all things are cyclical, even the idea that markets are not cyclical."

DARK POOL, *n.* An electronic trading network in which INSTITUTIONAL INVESTORs seek to buy or sell stocks without displaying their orders to the public (or "lit") market on a STOCK EXCHANGE. In theory, a dark pool prevents predatory traders from sniffing out large orders before they can be executed. In practice, dark pools can be teeming with HIGH-FREQUENCY TRADING sharks that snap between buyer and seller, capturing any pricing inefficiency for themselves.

DATA, *n.* The raw material from which Wall Street fabricates distortions for marketing purposes.

DAY TRADER, *n. See IDIOT.*

DEAD-CAT BOUNCE, *n.* A colorful piece of slang that makes market pundits sound as if they know what they are talking about when they don't. The term was popularized by financial analyst Raymond F. DeVoe, who said in 1986, "If you threw a dead cat off a 50-story building, it might bounce when it hit the sidewalk. But . . . it is still a dead cat." A

dead-cat bounce is thus a rise, believed to be only temporary, in the price of a financial asset that has been falling. It
is fairly easy to tell whether a cat is dead, but determining
whether a financial asset is dead is surprisingly difficult. A
dead-cat bounce could be the beginning of a roaring recovery, an inert nap, or a mangy decline.

DEFAULT, n. Also known as "de blame," or what borrower and lender alike will try to assign to each other as
soon as the borrower goes bust.

DERIVATIVE, n. Called "financial weapons of mass
destruction" by Warren Buffett, derivatives are assets linked
to, and deriving their value from, other assets. An OPTION
may derive its value from changes in the price of a STOCK;
futures contracts are derivatives on COMMODITIES or
currencies; swaps are derivatives based on interest rates or
another INDEX, and so forth. Derivatives are merely a tool;
just as knives can be used either to heal or to kill, derivatives
can either control risk or create it. The right derivative in
the right hands can reduce risk and augment return; in the
wrong hands, it can blow a portfolio to bits. Combined with
LEVERAGE, derivatives in the wrong hands can bring entire markets to the brink of thermonuclear meltdown.

DESIGNATION, n. A certificate and title vouching
that a financial advisor has learned something or other.
Some—like the CFA, or "chartered financial analyst"—
are so rigorous they require years of detailed study and
the equivalent of several college-level math and statistics
courses. Others, like the CFP, or "certified financial planner,"

require considerable preparation and knowledge. Many, however, require only that the advisor send in a check for a few hundred dollars and take an exam that the average cocker spaniel could pass.

There are hundreds of these cryptic acronyms in the financial industry, with more being foisted on the public every month.

> 💲 *A certificate framed as a plaque and hung on the wall behind the desk of Joel B. Poor, a financial advisor at the wealth-management firm of Trollope, Hooker, John & Ho, identifies Mr. Poor as having completed the rigorous coursework to earn the CBFD designation. Only by examining the fine print will a viewer learn what CBFD stands for: Certified Bearer of Financial Designations.*

Whenever a financial advisor boasts of his or her designations, remember that these are not graduate degrees; they may well be the equivalent of the correspondence classes that used to advertise on the inside of matchbook covers. And ask yourself: Why would people whose achievements, experience, and expertise are intrinsically impressive have to festoon their names with a string of incomprehensible acronyms?

DIP, *n.* and *v.* A decline in an asset's market price that has been brief and shallow, so far—as were the first few days of the Crash of 1929 and of the 2008–2009 global financial crisis. Although not all dips turn into disasters, nearly all disasters begin with a dip. Investors who believe that "buying the dips" is a recipe for success should be careful what they wish for; there may be more dips to buy than you have the willpower to withstand. *See also* CORRECTION.

DISCLOSURE, *n.* A statement that, by law, absolves a company of all responsibility—including any responsibility to present the statement in language that isn't so stupefyingly obscure that nobody can understand it. Intended to protect investors, disclosure instead protects the firms that issue it.

Most investors lack the time, expertise, or patience to read a 374-page PROSPECTUS or to comb through each line of a financial statement. And highly specific disclosures can lead to the conclusion that a warning such as "past performance is no guarantee of future results" means only that future profits aren't assured—when the real meaning is that past profits don't reduce the likelihood of future *losses.*

Extensive disclosures may lull investors into thinking that everything they need to know is contained in the prospectus itself—so they won't seek information from other, potentially contradictory sources. *See* CONFIRMATION BIAS.

The disclosure of multiple risks can have the perverse effect of making them seem less likely to transpire. By forcing issuers and banks to disclose every conceivable risk in excruciating detail, regulators frame those risks to investors as an enormous set of complex events—which therefore are harder to imagine occurring.

Disclosure is necessary, but it isn't sufficient. Telling investors everything they need to know, and having them understand any of it, are two very different things.

REGULATORs rely on disclosure as if it were a panacea, when in fact it is more like a Pandora's box.

DISCOUNT BROKERAGE, n. A firm that enables many investors to wreck their own portfolios instead of paying someone else to do it for them. Some of a discount brokerage's clients will use its convenience, efficiency, and low cost to build their wealth instead of impairing it; many, however, will trade themselves silly. Low commissions, paradoxically, are most valuable to those who incur them the least often.

DISCOUNTING, n. The impulsive process by which humans place a present value on future risks and rewards, making getting rich now feel better than getting even richer later. As the economist John Maynard Keynes wrote, "Human nature desires quick results, there is a peculiar zest in making money quickly, and remoter gains are discounted by the average man at a very high rate." Investors who don't discount the future too steeply—who have the patience and self-control to wait decades for gains to bear fruit—will prosper most in the long run.

DISPOSITION EFFECT, n. The tendency of investors to raise their tax bills and lower their investing returns by selling winning positions too soon while holding their losers too long. Because selling an investment has the finality of closing out a MENTAL ACCOUNT, most investors will prefer to sell quickly at a gain, enabling them to lock in a profit and create a source of pride. To sell a loser, however, is to lock in a loss, to foreclose any chance of future gain,

and to admit an irreversible error—so most investors sweep
their losers under the rug, keeping them while pretending
they aren't there. If one of these losers later turns out to
be profitable, you can disinter it and brag that you kept it
because you knew all along that it would be a big winner.
Being able to boast about that one will make up for the
money you are still losing on all the others.

DIVERSIFY, *v.* To own a variety of investments with
countervailing risks and returns, making your portfolio safer;
most investors, however, di-worse-ify instead, making their
portfolios more dangerous by buying lots of whatever has been
going up lately. If all your holdings go up together, they have
high CORRELATION and will also go down together. The
word "diversify" comes from the Latin *diversificare*, to make
different; to be diversified, you must own assets that sometimes make you feel good and sometimes make you feel bad.

DIVIDEND, *n.* In mathematics, "the number being divided by another," or the numerator of a fraction. In finance,
the proportion of a company's profits that it pays out to its
shareholders, or the sliver of a remnant.

DIVIDEND YIELD, *n.* A company's annual DIVI-
DEND divided by its current share price. "You buy a cow
for its milk and a stock for its yield," says an old Wall Street
proverb. But when a company gets into financial trouble and
has to cut its dividend to hoard cash for its own survival, the
yield will shrink or disappear. Investors who buy a stock *only*
for its yield may suddenly find themselves owning a cow that
gives no milk and is too scrawny to butcher for the meat.

DODD-FRANK ACT, *n.* A financial-regulation law, enacted in 2010, that sought to prevent financial institutions from becoming "too big to fail" but succeeded mainly at being too long to read, too complex to understand, and too convoluted to implement.

"A Jolly Dog," *Currier & Ives, lithograph, ca. 1878.* Library of Congress

DOG, *n.* The most disagreeable animal in the Wall Street menagerie; a stock that refuses to rise in price, obeying no command except "Down!" Every stock-market dog seems fun to play with at first but ends up biting BULLs and BEARs alike. Whoever coined the phrase "If you want a friend, get a dog" was unfamiliar with the canines of Wall Street.

DOLLAR-COST AVERAGING, *n.* Automatically investing on tiptoe; a procedure of using electronic transfers to invest a fixed amount of money into a mutual fund or other assets on a regular schedule, typically once a month. Because dollar-cost averaging eliminates the need for ad-hoc decisions about when or how much to buy, it takes most of the emotion out of investing—but not quite all.

As the great investor Benjamin Graham wrote in 1962: "Such a policy will pay off ultimately, regardless of when it is begun, *provided* that it is adhered to conscientiously and courageously under all intervening conditions. This is by no means a minor proviso. It presupposes that the dollar-cost averager will be a different sort of person from the rest of us, that he will not be subject to the alternations of exhilaration and deep gloom that have accompanied the gyrations of the stock market for generations past. This," concluded Graham, "I greatly doubt."

DOVE, *n.* A central banker who believes that an economy that hasn't responded to anything else the central bank has done will respond when it cuts interest rates. *See HAWK.*

DOWNSIDE PROTECTION, *n.* A tactic put in place by a financial advisor to protect against whatever hurt the value of a portfolio last time. The portfolio will be hurt by something entirely different next time, however.

DOWNSIDE RISK, *n.* The chance of losing money; the only kind of RISK there is, as no one seeks to avoid "upside risk," or making money. Unfortunately, many financial advisors who seek to minimize downside risk for their clients seem to end up eliminating any possible upside risk instead.

DRAWDOWN, *n.* A loss, measured from the highest to the lowest price, within a given period, often a month, quarter, or year. The *maximum drawdown* is the largest loss over any such period—so far, anyway.

Knowing how much you would have lost in the past gives you a rough sense of how much you might lose in the future, although the next drawdown can always turn out to be astoundingly large. Just as experienced homeowners know to double a contractor's estimate of what a renovation will cost in order to have a realistic expectation of the final total, investors would be wise to double the maximum historical drawdown and ask themselves whether they can handle a loss of that magnitude—before they invest.

DRY POWDER, *n*. In a PRIVATE-EQUITY FUND, the amount of cash available to be spent on acquiring companies for the portfolio. Any resemblance of this metaphor to dynamite in a barrel is, presumably, coincidental.

"*Guarding the Powder Kegs," Hans Sebald Beham, engraving, ca. 1510–1550.*
RIJKSMUSEUM

DUE DILIGENCE, *n*. The diligence that investors should do before committing any money to an investment. Gathering facts and marshaling common sense is hard work, however, so due diligence often goes undone.

A survey in 2007 of SOPHISTICATED INVESTORs found that many of them relied on their gut feelings about fund managers, didn't always run background checks on the managers or analyze a fund's financial statements, and were even willing to write multimillion-dollar checks without ever reading a fund's prospectus.

A few months later, Bernard Madoff's PONZI SCHEME was exposed, and "sophisticated investors" started doing a lot more homework. Their new commitment to due diligence was long overdue.

EARNINGS, *n.* Often called "the number," but only one of many numbers a company can choose to present reality. In theory, the earnings number is what is left over after the money that goes out is subtracted from the money that came in. In practice, earnings may be either understated (for instance, by owners who don't like to pay taxes or by managers who want future periods to look better by comparison) or overstated (by managers angling for big bonuses or seeking to placate impatient investors). Some executives seem to care less about managing their company than about managing their company's earnings.

EARNINGS SURPRISE, *n.* An outcome regarded as astounding on Wall Street even though it is merely the result of a force known to the rest of the world as "reality." After a company and the ANALYSTs who follow its stock spend months pretending they know precisely how much it will earn in the coming quarter, a bird from an endangered species gets electrocuted flying into wires at the company's factory in Utah or war breaks out in Lower Slobbovia, and the company suddenly has to pay $431 million to solve the problem. As a result, the company's earnings miss the CONSENSUS forecast. Often, an earnings surprise that is only one penny per share short of expectations can cause a stock to lose 20 percent or more in a few seconds. Although decades of data on hundreds of thousands of earnings forecasts show that analysts can't predict earnings within a mile, let alone within a penny, investors continue to be surprised when companies miss those forecasts. That is the biggest surprise of all.

EASY COMPS, *n.* Easy comparisons, or a fiscal quarter or year in which a company can resoundingly exceed its earnings in the prior period—because the earlier earnings were lousy. Often, the company made the easy comps possible by deliberately KITCHEN-SINKing the earnings in the earlier period.

EBITDA, *n.* Called "bullsh*t earnings" by the great investor Charles T. Munger, EBITDA is an acronym for "earnings before interest, tax, depreciation, and amortization," a method of reporting net income as if expenses like interest and taxes didn't matter. One company could spend twice as much on its borrowings as another and still report the same EBITDA. If Mr. Munger's term is too impolite for you, try thinking of EBITDA as standing for "earnings before including the decisive adjustments."

ECONOMIST, *n.* A professor who studies the real world from a perch in the ivory tower and concludes that the chaotic interactions of people, goods, and money conform to his or her theories. Some economists manage to construct theories so clever that they all come true, at least in the classroom. Because, in theory, there is no difference between theory and practice, economists get to proclaim that whatever works in the classroom must also work in the real world. But economic theorists who don't practice are "like eunuchs in a harem," the Harvard economist Alexander Gerschenkron once said. "They know everything about love, but they can't do anything about it."

EFFICIENT MARKET HYPOTHESIS, n. A theory in financial economics believed only by financial economists. In theory, the market price is the best estimate at any time of what securities are worth; it immediately incorporates all the relevant information available, as rational investors dynamically update their expectations to adjust to the latest events. In practice, however, investors either ignore new information or wildly overreact to it, regardless of how relevant it is. Even so, that doesn't make beating the market easy, because you must still outsmart tens of millions of other investors without incurring excess trading costs and taxes. As behavioral economist Meir Statman puts it, "The market may be crazy, but that doesn't make you a psychiatrist."

EMERGING MARKET, n. A country formerly described as part of "the Third World." Every five to ten years, stocks based in emerging-market countries become wildly popular for approximately eighteen months. At the beginning of that period, emerging-market stocks will be described as lower risk and faster growing than those based in advanced industrial economies. By the end of that period, after they collapse in price, emerging-market stocks will be described as higher risk and slower growing. At that point, the locals who sold the stocks to the foreigners will begin to buy them back.

ENDOWMENT, *n.* A pool of capital that helps fund the operations of an institution such as a university, a hospital, or a charitable foundation. Such an institution is expected to be perpetual, so the endowment is generally managed as if the next one to three years were all that mattered.

ENHANCED INDEXING, *n.* A technique that augments the returns of index funds—for the fund manager. Investors don't always share that experience. *See also SMART BETA.*

EQUITY, *n.* The ownership interest in a firm, often used as a synonym for "stock."
    Commonly believed to derive from the Latin *aequus,* for "equal" or "even," *equity* might be better thought of as deriving from the Latin *equus,* or "horse"—the rear end of which bears a close similarity to any investor who believes seriously that owning equity assures everyone equal treatment. *See CORPORATE GOVERNANCE.*

ETF, *n.* Acronym for "exchange-traded fund"; contrary to popular belief, not an acronym for "extremely tradable fund." ETFs (and their siblings ETNs, or "exchange-traded notes") track the returns of an INDEX, typically at very low cost. You could buy a handful of broadly diversified ETFs, hold them undisturbed for decades, and end up wealthy. But that would be boring, so instead many investors and financial advisors trade ETFs like mad. Thus, the investors enrich their brokers, the financial advisors enrich themselves, and the markets do what they have always done and always will: transfer wealth from those who trade to those who wait.

Incapable of leaving well enough alone, Wall Street has taken the good idea of ETFs and complicated them until many have become a bad idea. Increasingly, ETFs trading thousands of times a day own assets that might not trade at all that day. And you can buy *inverse ETFs*, which move in the opposite direction of the daily return of the INDEX they are tied to, and even *leveraged inverse ETFs*, which move twice or triple the opposite of an index. A triple-leveraged inverse ETF, for instance, would gain 3 percent on a day when its underlying index loses 1 percent and lose 3 percent on a day when the index gains 1 percent. Such funds are suitable only for the kind of person who might enjoy getting orthopedic surgery without anesthesia.

> $ *"We think this ETF is extremely safe,"* said Karen Little, a partner at the wealth-management firm of Flynt, Sparks & Asch in Las Vegas, Nevada. *"It's designed to go up when small stocks with high dividends trading in Tanzania go down, and to go down when they go up. In fact, it will move twice as much as they do every day! So it won't behave anything like US stocks or bonds, and that will make your overall portfolio safer."*

EX-DIVIDEND, *adj.* Not, as you might guess, a former or deceased dividend; rather, an indication that on or after the *ex-dividend date*, the buyer of a stock or mutual fund is not entitled to receive the next DIVIDEND payment. *See also* X.

EXCHANGE, *n. See STOCK EXCHANGE.*

EXCHANGE-TRADED FUND, *n. See ETF.*

EXECUTION, n. The act of inflicting capital punishment by putting a prisoner to death; the fulfillment by a brokerage firm of a customer's order to buy or sell a security. These two uses of the same word have absolutely nothing in common, according to the brokerage industry.

EXPECTED RETURN, n. The anticipated growth rate of the value of an asset, typically set by the fevered imagination of investors at approximately twice what the actual return will turn out to be. When performance turns out to be much lower, investors throw a tantrum, pick up their toys, and go home.

If, instead, investors expected to earn a return *lower* than past performance implies, they would be much more capable of staying the course when short-term results are poor. As G. K. Chesterton wrote: "It is commonly in a somewhat cynical sense that men have said, 'Blessed is he who expecteth nothing, for he shall not be disappointed.' It was in a wholly happy and enthusiastic sense that St. Francis said, 'Blessed is he who expecteth nothing, for he shall enjoy everything.'"

EXPUNGE, v. To wipe the slate clean, so a broker's publicly available record doesn't show all the disciplinary actions that have been taken against him or her. From the Latin *ex*, or "out," and *pungere*, "to prick, to puncture, to punch a hole into." When interviewing brokers or financial advisors, it is a good idea to ask whether anything has been expunged from their disclosure forms.

FAIR-VALUE PRICING, *n.* A guess.

FAIRNESS OPINION, *n.* A detailed analysis of a pending transaction, prepared by an investment bank, concluding whatever the people who commissioned it want to hear. If the bank prepares the fairness opinion for a potential buyer, it will conclude that the buying price is fair. If the bank prepares it for a potential seller, the opinion will conclude that the selling price is fair.

FALLEN ANGEL, *n.* A formerly high-flying stock that has crashed to earth, or a bond once regarded as high quality that now trades as a JUNK BOND. The image derives from the Christian belief, dramatized in John Milton's *Paradise Lost*, that rebellious angels are expelled or flung from Heaven as punishment for their treason against God. As a financial term, *fallen angel* appears to have originated in the wake of the 1973–1974 market crash, when many MOMENTUM stocks fell by 80 percent or more. Investors often buy a fallen angel in the belief that it will rise again, although it is a long way back to financial Heaven once a stock or bond falls to earth.

FALLING KNIFE, *n.* An asset whose price is plunging so hard that if you catch it, it will cut right through you. It might then take a DEAD-CAT BOUNCE or turn into a FALLEN ANGEL. Trying to predict which will happen will help you pass the time while you bandage your hands.

Investors often believe that an asset that has already fallen 90 percent can only fall 10 percent more. Not so: A stock that starts at $100 and falls 90 percent to $10 can easily fall another 90 percent to $1. It can then fall another 90 percent to 10 cents. After that, it can fall *another* 90 percent to 1 cent, and it still might not be done. Falling knives can fall faster and farther than you might ever believe until you finally catch one and feel it yourself.

FAT-FINGER TRADE, *n.* A multimillion-dollar typo; an erroneous order originating on the institutional trading desk of a major bank or brokerage when an employee strikes the wrong spot on a computer keyboard. Fat-finger trades can result in buying when a firm meant to sell, selling when it meant to buy, trading the wrong amount of the right security, or trading the right amount of the wrong security.

FEE, *n.* A tiny word with a teeny sound, which nevertheless is the single-biggest determinant of success or failure for most investors.

Investors who keep fees as low as possible will, on average, earn the highest possible returns. The opposite may be true for their financial advisors, although that is still not widely understood.

As the popular financial journalist M. T. Head recently wrote:

"Man and Devil Filling Sack with
Money," Willem Swanenburgh after
Maarten van Heemskerck, engraving,
1609. Rijksmuseum

$ *"We think 1 percent a year is a very reasonable fee, given how hard we work for our clients," said wealth manager Bill Muchmore of Adenauer Doe & Co. Asked why the sound of waves breaking on a beachfront seemed to be audible in the background during our conversation, Mr. Muchmore hastened to explain that he was walking back to his office from lunch and several city buses had just passed by him.*

FIDUCIARY DUTY, *n.* The requirement that financial advice should be at least as good for the person receiving it as for the person providing it—an idea so radical that Wall Street is attacking it with every weapon in its arsenal. If BROKERS became subject to a fiduciary duty, they would no longer be able to charge high fees to put their own interests ahead of their clients'. That, according to the brokerage industry, would force many investors to make their own decisions for free—which would somehow leave these investors worse off than before. If you don't find that at least slightly confusing, you haven't been paying attention.

FINANCIAL ADVISOR, *n.* Often, someone who cares deeply about being prudent, diligent, competent, and honest, in which case his or her services will be priceless; sometimes, someone who cares only about being a BIG PRODUCER, in which case you are in for big trouble.

FINANCIAL JOURNALIST, *n.* Someone who is an expert at moving words about markets around on a page or screen until they sound impressive, regardless of whether they mean anything.

Until the early twentieth century, financial journalists often knew exactly what they were doing, as many of them were paid overtly or covertly by market manipulators to promote or trash various investments. As William Armstrong wrote in 1848 in his pamphlet "Stocks and Stock-Jobbing in Wall-Street," most stock-market journalism of the day was produced "by individuals who are bribed to write in a specified manner." Matthew Hale Smith, in his 1875 book, *Bulls and Bears of New York*, pointed out that the official pressroom for reporters covering the stock market was in the headquarters of Henry Clews & Co., a leading investment bank. Other early financial journalists, including Mark Twain, regularly touted stocks they owned, hoping to run the share price up with their puffery.

Nowadays, most financial journalists are honest, which is progress—and ignorant, which isn't.

FINE, n. and v. The monetary equivalent of trying to stop a pack of rampaging wolves by tugging on their whiskers. Penalties for unethical or improper conduct meant to deter similar behavior in the future, fines are a minor irritant on Wall Street, regarded as part of the normal cost of doing business, like sales taxes or highway tolls, usually amounting to only a few days' worth of profits. Like "finish" and "final," the word "fine" is rooted in the Latin *finis*, or end. But on Wall Street, fines often mark a beginning rather than an end.

> $ *"The six largest US financial companies have paid more than $128 billion in fines related to the financial crisis," said Vera Pawling, chief executive officer of Aiken,*

Paine, Hertz & Co., the second-biggest bank. "That is
more than nine months' worth of total net profit!" she
added indignantly. "Mistakes were made, and the lessons
have been learned. It's time for politicians, regulators, and
the public to stop the retribution."

FIRE SALE, *n.* and *adj.* The sale of an asset at a scorched price by someone who not long ago was burning to buy it.

FIXED INCOME, *n.* Income that is fixed to vary just when the investor least expects it to.

FLASH CRASH, *n.* A severe and almost instantaneous drop in a financial market, originally used to describe the events of May 6, 2010, when HIGH-FREQUENCY TRADING firms filled orders at such rapidly falling prices that the market collapsed around them. The Dow Jones Industrial Average fell roughly 600 points, or nearly 6 percent, in four and a half minutes. In some of the fastest and wildest fluctuations of stock prices ever seen, more than 20,000 trades were filled at prices at least 60 percent above or below where they had stood a few seconds earlier; some stocks sold for 99 percent less than their previous price, while others traded at up to $100,000 a share. Twenty minutes later, prices were right back to where they had been.

The flash crash of 2010 was not the first; on May 28, 1962, many stocks fell roughly 10 percent in less than twelve minutes, and the Dow lost 5.7 percent for the day. Nor will it be the last.

FLIGHT TO SAFETY, *n.* A mass movement among investors that typically occurs almost immediately after a flight of fancy. Having deluded themselves into thinking that risk had been repealed, investors now scurry to dump the dangerous junk they recently bought and to replace it with safer assets like US Treasury debt. Flights to safety typically hit the runway after most of the risk has already been expelled from the market.

FOCUS, FOCUSED FUND, *n. See BEST-IDEAS FUND.*

FORECASTING, *n.* The attempt to predict the unknowable by measuring the irrelevant; a task that, in one way or another, employs most people on Wall Street.

Because the human mind hates admitting the truth that the world is largely random and unpredictable, forecasters will always be in demand, regardless of their futility. Wall Street follows what marketing professor J. Scott Armstrong has called the seer-sucker theory: "For every seer there is a sucker."

In the real world, as with weather forecasts or predictions about who will win a sporting event, those making the projections typically estimate the likelihood that they are correct. Wall Street forecasts, on the other hand, almost never have probabilities attached. As decision scientist Baruch Fischhoff wrote in 1994, "When both forecaster and client exaggerate the quality of forecasts, the client will often win the race to the poorhouse." *See also OUTLOOK.*

FORTUNE, *n.* Wealth; also, luck.

Both meanings derive from Fortuna, the capricious and unappeasable Roman goddess of change. For most of the past two millennia, the two meanings weren't merely interchangeable; they were one and the same. Wealth was understood to be largely the result of luck, and luck was the substrate of wealth. As a result, money was regarded as ephemeral. Your fortune was effectively on loan to you from the goddess Fortuna, who could call her property back from you at any

"Wheel of Fortune,"
Franco-Dutch illuminated
manuscript, early
fifteenth century.
THE BRITISH LIBRARY

time and without warning. The Wheel of Fortune was indistinguishable from the Circle of Life.

For centuries, Fortune was portrayed spinning a wheel and often standing on a sphere, ball, or bubble, symbolizing her own precarious balance. Each person's life, luck, and wealth thus played out as a tug-of-war with Fortune, who would whirl people from top to bottom and back again whenever she was bored or angry. Artists often showed her spinning her great wheel one-quarter turn at a time toward the left (*sinistra* in Latin), symbolizing the evil turn that her judgments often took. Sometimes a king tried to cling to the wheel as she cranked it. He typically called out, "I will reign" from the ascending side of the wheel, "I reign" at the top, "I have reigned" on the way down, and "I have no reign" at the bottom. Our modern idiom "to come full circle" is a vestige of this view of fortune.

Only after the Enlightenment began to exalt the power of the individual mind did it seem feasible for people to "make" their own fortune rather than merely having it on loan from a fickle goddess. Even as late as 1835, you can hear the echoes of Fortuna in the words of Nathan Mayer Rothschild, then the world's most powerful financier: "It requires a great deal of boldness and a great deal of caution to make a great fortune; and when you have got it, it requires ten times as much wit to keep it."

Something was gained and something was lost in the Industrial Revolution, when people finally outgrew the ancient belief that luck and wealth were one and the same: entrepreneurship became possible, and hubris became an epidemic. As almost everyone came to believe that he or she could make a fortune, it became increasingly difficult to remember that making and keeping wealth is impossible without luck.

Investors who forget this lesson so deeply rooted in the historical meaning of the word *fortune* will have to learn it for themselves. They are most likely to learn how ephemeral fortune can be, and how much it depends upon luck, just after they become convinced that it is permanent and that they derived it from their own skill.

FULCRUM FEE, *n.* An arrangement—so sensible that it is almost never offered—under which an investment firm charges clients a higher percentage fee when it outperforms the market than when it underperforms. Most firms instead charge the same percentage fees regardless of whether their performance is terrific or terrible. Even more strangely, clients willingly agree to pay this way. The clients are thereby betting that the money manager can beat the market even though the firm is refusing to gamble its own fees on its future performance. Whose bet do you think is more likely to pay off?

GAAP, *abbr. n.* Rules—Generally Accepted Accounting Principles, pronounced "gap"—that permit companies to prepare their financial statements with only a tenuous connection to reality. The managers of some companies view GAAP "not as a standard to be met, but as an obstacle to overcome," Warren Buffett has written. "Too often their accountants willingly assist them. ('How much,' says the client, 'is two plus two?' Replies the cooperative accountant, 'What number did you have in mind?')"

GAIN, *v.* To earn an imaginary profit on paper, savored temporarily before it turns into an actual loss. In one of the primary paradoxes of finance, those who pursue gains with the greatest intensity are the least likely to achieve them; those who wait patiently for them are the most likely to receive them. *See LOSE.*

GO-ANYWHERE FUND, *n.* A mutual fund, specializing in stocks or a wider range of assets, that can lose money in every imaginable way—and then some. *See also UNCONSTRAINED BOND FUND.*

GO DARK, *v.* To stop filing the financial statements with the Securities and Exchange Commission that previously shed so much light on the company's health; also, to withdraw stock from trading on an exchange. Henceforth, investors will just have to guess how the company is doing—as opposed to whatever it was they were doing before.

GOLD, *n.* What people think they will make piles of when they buy a shiny yellow metal that is useful primarily for melting into cuff links and charm bracelets.

GOLDBUG, *n.* Someone who thinks everything will make the price of gold go up—someday.

GOLDEN PARACHUTE, *n.* Although gold is extremely heavy, a parachute made of this substance nonetheless assures the wearer of a soft and comfortable landing even when flung in disgrace from the commanding heights of corporate headquarters. A CEO bailing out of the company with a golden parachute may be awarded hundreds of millions of dollars by the board of directors, mainly to express the board's gratitude that the CEO is finally leaving and that the money to get rid of him or her comes from the shareholders rather than out of their own pockets.

GREATER FOOL THEORY, *n.* The belief that no matter how foolish a price you pay for a stock or other asset, you can always find a greater fool who will pay more to buy it from you. Why bother figuring out what a stock is worth, when you can simply gamble that somebody else will think it's worth even more?

The term has been traced back to the 1960s, although the hope of always being able to sell to someone even more reckless than you are is almost certainly as old as financial markets themselves.

It might seem surprising that there could ever be a shortage of fools in this world, but if you count on always finding one just when you most need to, you will wake up one day to find that everyone else has suddenly smartened up and the greater fool is you.

GREECE, *n.* A nation in southern Europe famous for philosophy, mathematics, architecture, and shortchanging its creditors. Greece was in default or behind on its debt in 51 percent of the years between 1826 and 2008, according to economists Carmen Reinhart and Kenneth Rogoff. Nevertheless, professional investors rushed to buy Greek bonds in the late 2000s. When Greece defaulted again in 2012, these "experts" were astonished—even though the average seven-year-old would have advised against lending money to a borrower with such a history.

GREEN SHOE, *n.* and *adj.* The option for an investment bank to offer more securities than planned, in order to meet excess demand from investors; believed to derive from the Green Shoe Co., whose IPO in 1960 was so hot that its bankers had to buy more shares from the company to fill extra orders. Investors should always remember that they won't go barefoot if they can't buy into a green-shoe offering.

GREENMAIL, *n.* and *v.* A cross between greenbacks and blackmail, greenmail is paid when a company targeted for a hostile takeover buys out the stockholdings of the bidder for more than the current market price. The underperforming managers of the takeover target keep their jobs and their outlandish pay, while the takeover bidder earns a quick killing without having to do the work of turning around a struggling company. The remaining outside shareholders, however, are usually left owning a business with lousy management and even less cash than before.

"Oleum Olivarum," Philips Galle after
Jan van der Straet, engraving, ca. 1595.
RIJKSMUSEUM

GRIND, *v.* To move slowly and with difficulty, as in "prices will grind higher" or "yields are grinding lower." If the image above gives you the impression that the financial markets are gigantic millstones that slowly revolve and crush most investors who attempt to outsmart them, you are not far off.

GROSS SPREAD, *n.* The portion of the total proceeds of a securities underwriting earned as FEEs by the investment banks that managed the offering—often up to 7 percent of the total, a spread that is gross indeed.

HAIRCUT, *n.* Sometimes just a trim, at other times a scalping; the difference between the reported VALUE of an investment and its PRICE when it is sold or when reality forces a reappraisal, whichever comes first.

HALO EFFECT, *n.* The tendency of one judgment to cast a warm glow (or dark cloud) over other related factors. If the price of a company's stock has gone up strongly, the people who run the company will seem almost superhuman. In early 2000, for instance, with Cisco Systems' stock up more than 100,000 percent over the previous decade, *Fortune* magazine called its chief executive, John Chambers, "the world's greatest CEO." A year later, with the stock down almost 80 percent, *Fortune* described Chambers as having been dangerously blind to signs of the coming collapse. The same company run by the same man seemed utterly transformed as soon as its stock price fell. One way to counteract the halo effect is to use a CHECKLIST to consider each aspect of a company separately.

THE DEVIL'S FINANCIAL DICTIONARY   101

HANDLE, *n*. In the real world, handles are used to get a secure grip on something, a love handle, for example. On Wall Street, handles are the whole-integer part of a market price; a stock trading at $30.48, for instance, has a "30-handle." But financial handles often slip through your fingers as soon as you try to hold onto them; a 30-handle can become a 20-handle or a 10-handle in a hurry.

HAPPINESS LETTER, *n*. A seemingly innocuous letter sent to a brokerage client whenever a mandatory periodic review turns up risky, inappropriate, or excessive trading, such as a predatory broker trading the account as if his underpants were on fire. If the client doesn't respond with a written statement of dissatisfaction, then he or she is deemed "happy." Should a legal dispute later arise, the firm will claim that the client had the chance to highlight any problems and chose not to do so—which often will be regarded as confirmation that the firm did nothing wrong.

HAWK, *n*. A central banker who believes that an economy that hasn't responded to anything else the central bank has done will respond when it raises interest rates. *See DOVE.*

HEAD AND SHOULDERS, *n*. A purported pattern in TECHNICAL ANALYSIS in which the price of a stock or other asset bounces up a little, down a little, up a lot, down a lot, up a little, then down a little—which is supposed to mean a lot about how the price will move in the future. If that reminds you of the lyrics to the children's song,

Eyes and ears and mouth and nose,
Head, shoulders, knees and toes, knees and toes,

you might well be right, but you have no future as a technical analyst.

HEADLINE, *adj.* Whatever a trader will instantly seize upon in a government or company announcement as meaningful, even though it probably isn't in the short term and certainly isn't in the long term. In the real world, "headline" is a noun, referring to the large type at the top of an article announcing what it is about. On Wall Street, it is an adjective, as in "headline inflation," "headline jobs report," and "headline number." *Headline risk* is the chance that news coverage will crush the price of a stock or other asset when traders panic over the negative news. The terms are often used to convey that distinctive I-know-more-than-you-do feeling:

> 💲 *"The headline number wasn't good," said Loren D. Barr, an analyst at the investment-banking firm of Ely, Griese & Luby, "but once you dug into the release there was a lot to be bullish about."*

HEDGE FUND, *n.* Expensive and exclusive funds numbering in the thousands, of which only about a hundred might be run by managers talented enough to beat the market with consistency and low risk. "The rest," says the financial journalist Morgan Housel, "charge ten times the fees of mutual funds for half the performance of index funds, pay half the income-tax rates of taxi drivers, and have triple the ego of rock stars."

Historically, hedge funds were highly secretive, seldom disclosing what they owned and barely deigning to describe their overall strategy. That mystique made them especially attractive to SOPHISTICATED INVESTORs—much the way nearly everyone prefers to receive presents covered in opaque wrapping paper.

Hedge funds date back at least to the 1920s, when they were called "hedged funds" after the ancient practice of planting hedges around a property to deter outside threats.

The term "to hedge" or "to hedge in" has been commonly used in English since at least the seventeenth century to describe the act of making an offsetting bet to compensate for possible loss on a speculation.

The origins of the word have other implications for investors. The use of *hedge* in English to mean a fence or defensive barrier dates back approximately a millennium. As a verb, the word has had a variety of related meanings: By the mid-1500s, to *hedge in* meant "to enclose, to prevent escape or free movement" and "to shut out or exclude"; in the seventeenth century, it also meant "to monopolize, to restrict for one's own use" and to increase the likelihood of being repaid on a debt by folding it into a larger obligation that was better secured.

Hedge funds are often set up to be just as difficult to sell as they are to buy, thus hedging their own wealthy clients in while hedging out most potential investors. A hedge fund often makes so much money for its managers that it ends up holding their capital almost exclusively, as the insiders' wealth crowds out all the other clients combined. Finally, hedge funds that take on too much risk may end up being folded into other, larger portfolios run by the same firm. All these outcomes lurk within the forgotten historical meanings of the word *hedge*.

In theory, hedge funds should enable skilled managers to perform brilliantly without the distractions of frequent disclosure or fickle inflows and outflows of money from the investing public. And some have capitalized on their structure to achieve stunning track records. But most haven't.

In recent years, the typical hedge fund has done less hedging of its bets, concentrating them instead. The result, on average, has been poor, leading to common statements like "hedge-fund performance has been terrible." That is incorrect; the performance of hedge-fund *investors* has been terrible, while the returns (in the form of fees) for hedge-fund *managers* have remained lavish.

Hedge funds are often called an ASSET CLASS, implying that they offer a combination of risk and reward distinctly different from that of stocks or bonds. In fact, what is distinctly different is their fees, typically up to 2 percent of the total invested assets and 20 percent of any profits. Rounding the numbers a little, a $10-billion hedge fund that earns a 10 percent return will generate more than $400 million in fees for the manager. The fee would be the same even if the stock market rose 20 percent and the fund thus underperformed by a margin of two to one.

Unsurprisingly, the biggest investors in many a hedge fund are the managers themselves. They have to put all that fee income somewhere.

Flappers Doing the Charleston,
photograph, 1920. LIBRARY OF CONGRESS

HEMLINE THEORY, *n.* The belief—popularized by male traders on Wall Street, who have only two things on their minds (money is one)—that stock prices rise when the hemlines of women's dresses go up and fall when hemlines lengthen.

If the theory is correct, then short skirts mean you should go LONG on stocks; long skirts mean you should go SHORT on stocks. Hemlines, the theory says, were long in the 1930s and 1940s, when stocks also fell toward the floor; hemlines were short in the 1920s, when flappers ruled fashion and BULLS ruled the stock market. And hot pants were all the rage in 1971, when stocks gained 14.3 percent in the United States.

But the miniskirt was popular in the mid-1960s, when stocks bounced all over the place. And maxiskirts came back in vogue in 2010, just in time for a roaring bull market.

The theory unravels completely if you try to account for stock returns in the nineteenth century, when hemlines never rose above the ankle. And if you want to end up in stitches, try explaining markets like those in Dubai or Kuwait, where stock prices are wildly volatile even though women's hemlines haven't budged in centuries. All the hemline theory proves is that Wall Street loves spurious correlations, or variables that appear to move together even if randomness is the only plausible explanation.

HERDING, *n.* The tendency of investors to ignore what's cheap and act like sheep, moving together in a flock rather than thinking for themselves. There is safety in numbers, so investors buy assets not because they are undervalued but merely because "everyone else" is buying them, and sell not because something fundamental has changed but because "everyone else" is selling.

Herding is common among individual investors; security analysts, government-

"Two Fools Dancing,"
Hendrick Hondius after
Pieter Bruegel the Elder,
engraving, 1642. RIJKSMUSEUM

bond traders, professional futures traders, mutual-fund managers, hedge-fund managers, and the biggest buyers of exchange-traded funds; within industrial sectors of the stock market; and across stock markets around the world. Investors herded into technology stocks in 1999 and out of them in 2000; into real estate and financial stocks in 2007 and out in 2008; into gold in 2011 and out by 2014. Before that, they herded into the NIFTY FIFTY stocks in 1972 and out in 1973–1974; into computer and education stocks in 1968 and out in 1969; into uranium and bowling and aeronautics stocks in the 1950s and then right out; into utility stocks and investment trusts in 1928 and out in 1929; and so forth and so on, with numbing repetition, back into the mists of markets immemorial.

Somehow it seems altogether fitting that the first known market forecasters, the BARUs of ancient Mesopotamia, tried predicting what was to come by examining the livers of sheep.

See also CONTRARIAN; ROTATION.

HEURISTICS, *n.* Mental shortcuts, such as ANCHOR-ING, AVAILABILITY, and REPRESENTATIVENESS, that substitute intuition for analysis based on probabilities and statistical evidence; from the Greek *eureka*, "I have found it." In the short run, people who invest on the basis of heuristics have all the fun; in the long run, those who invest on the basis of statistics amass all the wealth.

HFT, *abbr. n. See HIGH-FREQUENCY TRADING.*

HIGH-FREQUENCY TRADING, *n.* A technique often used to cheat other traders by a few fractions of a penny in a few millionths of a second, much faster than deceptive trading used to be. The practice of snooping on stock quotes and using private information to trade ahead of others is as old as Wall Street itself. High-frequency trading became controversial only after it was based on advanced computer technology rather than cheating by hand.

In 1790, high-frequency traders cashed in on Alexander Hamilton's proposal to restructure the federal debt by hiring fast ships to outrace the spread of the news on land. That enabled the traders to snap up US bonds at bargain prices from holders who were still in the dark.

Around 1835, reporter Daniel H. Craig began boarding steamships in Halifax, Nova Scotia. He swiftly digested the financial news in the European newspapers on board, then recorded it in tiny bulletins on tissue paper that he strapped to the feet of trained carrier pigeons. As each ship approached Boston, Craig released the birds, which homed in on his office, where clerks transcribed the news and distributed it to high-frequency traders who paid up to $500 for each hour they were able to get it ahead of the general public.

One of the earliest known books on the US stock market, Frederick Jackson's *A Week in Wall Street by One Who Knows*, published in 1841, describes a high-frequency trader nicknamed "Mr. Eavesdropper," who put his ear to the keyhole of the door of the stock exchange, "and before the transactions of the board were publicly known, he had privately contracted for the delivery of a large number of shares." During the Civil War, brokers who weren't members of the New York Stock Exchange paid as much as $100 per day for the similar privilege of using an annex known as Goodwin's Room to spy on activity in the main trading hall.

In the 1980s and 1990s, investment banks ran "upstairs markets" in which they traded large blocks of stock for INSTITUTIONAL INVESTORs and were commonly believed to buy or sell the same stocks for themselves first, capturing the difference as profit. Such "front-running" was rarely detected or punished, however.

For decades, trading intermediaries called "specialists" or "market makers" shaved at least 12.5 cents off every trade for themselves. The take of today's high-frequency traders appears to average 1 cent or less. Their equipment is much faster than it was in the 1790s, but the techniques some high-frequency traders use are just electronic updates of the same old dirty tricks.

HIGH-NET-WORTH INVESTOR, *n.* Often abbreviated as HNWI, which should logically be pronounced *honey,* as in "honey pot"; the term that brokers, financial advisors, fund companies, and WEALTH MANAGERs use to describe someone whose assets can yield a gusher of fees.

An "ultra-high-net-worth investor" (or UHNWI, which ought to be pronounced *You honey!*) is someone who can generate hundreds of thousands or even millions of dollars in annual fees.

Various firms require as little as $500,000 or as much as $2 million in assets to qualify for high-net-worth status, and anywhere between $5 million and $100 million to hit the ultra-high-net-worth cutoff. Millions of dollars in assets can generate tens of thousands of dollars a year in fees.

You could just call these folks "rich people," of course, but that would be crass—and poor marketing. It's always easier to pick someone's pocket when you use jargon to make that person feel like part of a private club whose members have especially fine pockets.

> $ "*I must remind you that we provide the ultimate in service for our ultra-high-net-worth clients,*" *said Lincoln Towne-Carr, a senior partner at the wealth-management firm of Markham, Ketchum, Yoakum & Burnham. "Would you like a complimentary glass of sixty-year-old sherry from our private winery in Jerez de Frontera, Spain?" He paused, then added with a twinkle in his eye: "You have earned it, after all."*

HIGH-YIELD BONDS, *n. See JUNK BONDS.*

HINDENBURG OMEN, *n.* An indicator in TECHNICAL ANALYSIS that has predicted approximately 548 of the past three market crashes. It is calculated by establish-

"*The Hindenburg Burning," photograph, 1937.* US NAVY

ing whether the daily number of new fifty-two-week highs is no more than twice the daily number of new fifty-two-week lows, then determining that the daily number of new fifty-two-week highs and the daily number of fifty-two-week lows is each at least 2.5 percent (or 2.8 percent or 2.2 percent, depending on whom you ask) of the total number of stocks that either go up or down, *if and only if* (1) stocks overall are higher than they were ten weeks ago and (2) the exponential moving average of the daily ordinal difference of advances minus declines over the past nineteen trading days is less than the exponential moving average of the daily ordinal difference of advances minus declines over the past thirty-nine trading days.

If you were able to read that in one breath, you are qualified to become either a pearl diver or one of those people who read the disclaimers in automobile commercials on the radio.

For some peculiar reason, the Hindenburg omen is named after a gas-filled blimp that exploded and burned in 1937.

HINDSIGHT BIAS, *n.* Only perhaps a half-dozen market pundits saw the financial crisis coming before 2008, but you can't swing a Hermès necktie on Wall Street without hitting someone who claims to have predicted it. That is typical of hindsight bias, the mechanism in the human mind that makes surprises vanish. Once you learn what did happen, your mind tricks you into believing that you always knew it would happen. Contrary to the popular cliché, hindsight is not 20/20; it is barely better than legally blind. If you don't record and track your forecasts, you shouldn't say that you knew all along what would happen in the end. And if you can't review all the predictions of pundits, you should never believe that they foresaw the future. *See also CERTAINTY; CLEARLY; FORECASTING; MEMORY.*

HOME BIAS, *n.* The tendency of investors to prefer buying STOCKS headquartered near their houses, as if being within driving distance could somehow make companies safer. Even the managers of MUTUAL FUNDS and pension

plans behave like this. But, at least in the STOCK MAR-
KET, there are many places like home—often providing
higher return at lower risk. DIVERSIFYing geographically
always makes sense, wherever you happen to live. *See also*
ILLUSION OF CONTROL.

HOSTILE TAKEOVER, *n. See TENDER OFFER.*

HOT, *adj.* Formerly hot. As surely as the sun will set in the
west, investors will be offered the chance to buy a hot asset
only as it is about to turn cold.

IDIOT, *n. See DAY TRADER.*

ILLUSION OF CONTROL, *n.* The belief that the superstitious rituals of a single individual can counteract the randomness that dominates the universe. Gamblers blow on their dice, shake them longer, or throw them harder when they want a high number; lottery players will play only when they can select their own "lucky numbers"; and investors who pick their own stocks or funds expect higher returns than those whose investments are selected for them by someone else. If traders are on a losing streak, they will wear the same suit or tie they had on the last time they made money, check prices even more often than usual, postpone a vacation, or refuse to write with a red pen. Herbert McDade III, the former president of Lehman Brothers, used to put his car in the same parking space each day the market was going up. That, however, did not keep Lehman Brothers from going under and declaring bankruptcy in 2008.

INCOME STATEMENT, *n.* The part of a company's financial statements in which it may exaggerate its income and understate its expenses.

INCUBATE, *v.* To test a MUTUAL FUND in private, with money only from the firm that runs the fund—giving the portfolio the unusual advantages of great flexibility and very small size. If it works, the company will launch the fund after a year and attract swarms of new investors by promoting its one-year track record of "outperformance." If it fails, the firm will shut the fund down and no one will be the wiser.

INDENTURE, *n.* From the Latin *dentem*, "tooth," a document that stipulates all the obligations and conditions under which a bond issuer borrows money. As some JUNK BOND purchasers in recent years have discovered when they realized too late that their indentures lacked any bite at all, these documents should—but do not always—put teeth into creditors' claims.

Massachusetts-Bay Bond with Indentures, 1777.
MUSEUM OF AMERICAN FINANCE

In medieval Europe, for security, each party to a legal or financial agreement insisted that the document be written in duplicate on a single piece of parchment or vellum that was then cut in two with a toothed pattern. That prevented forgeries or illicit alterations of the terms: Whenever a dispute arose or the contract expired, the two parts of the document would be authenticated by touching them together to confirm that the indentures, or "teeth," meshed perfectly.

The indentures cut into documents were shaped like incisors, presumably to remind the participants of their bite. With the passage of time, they became less toothlike; by the eighteenth century, they were gentle scallops or waves, and by the late nineteenth century, they had disappeared. Only the name "indenture" remains, and the bite is often gone, too.

INDEX, *n.* Derived from the Latin for "forefinger," a measure of the stock market, bond market, or other basket of financial assets that enables clients to point a finger at professional investors who can't match its performance.

By extension, the word *index* means a sign or guiding principle; the word *indicate* shares the same root. Among the earliest major financial indexes were the Dow Jones 11-stock average (later the Dow Jones Industrial Average) and the Standard Statistics Co. Composite (later the S&P 500 Index), dating to 1884 and 1923, respectively.

INDEX FUND, *n.* A type of MUTUAL FUND or EXCHANGE-TRADED FUND run by a machine that makes the humans who run ACTIVE funds look like monkeys. Effectively owning all the stocks or bonds in an INDEX, the index fund doesn't try to outsmart the market; it tries to *be* the market. Unlike an active manager who assumes that tens of millions of other investors are all wrong, the index fund is built on the assumption that the market price is usually the best guess of what securities are worth. Because index funds are extremely cheap and generate paltry trading commissions, Wall Street scorns them with the phrase "Why settle for average?" The answer: year after year, index funds outperform the majority of active funds, at far lower cost.

> $ *"Index funds aren't good enough for our clients," said Robin M. Daley, chief executive officer of the brokerage firm Putnam, Woods, Greene, Bunker & Parr, at a securities-industry dinner last week. "We feel the same way," replied Justin Abel, president of Stoller Cash & Rector, the wealth-management firm. "Where do you put your own money, Robin?" he asked. "You've got to be kidding," replied Mr. Daley, puffing on his Cohiba cigar. "All my money's in index funds." Mr. Abel took another sip of 1982 Bordeaux and nodded: "Mine, too."*

INDIVIDUAL INVESTOR, *n.* Someone who, without wise advice, is likely to ruin a small portfolio, generally $1 million or less. *See also INSTITUTIONAL INVESTOR; RETAIL INVESTOR.*

INFLATION, *n.* The process by which money loses its purchasing power, becoming worth less over time—and worthless, sometimes. Inflation is typically caused when a government tries to solve particular economic problems by burying them in newly printed money—thereby creating much worse problems by making daily life unaffordable, especially for the poor. As the comedian Henny Youngman said, "Americans are getting stronger. Twenty years ago, it took two people to carry ten dollars' worth of groceries. Today, a five-year-old can do it."

INSIDE INFORMATION, *n.* Information that could put you inside a prison. If you work at a hedge fund, however, it might take a few years for that to happen, and you should be able to stash away several million dollars in the meantime. And the legal definitions of inside information vary so widely that no one—including judges, law professors, and regulators—is sure what it is.

> $ *Federal prosecutors today grilled a hedge-fund analyst during the insider-trading trial currently underway in US District Court in Manhattan. The analyst had bought 100,000 shares of Quadruple Helix Corp., a company developing new techniques for cloning, less than fifteen seconds after concluding a call with the wife of Quadruple Helix's chief financial officer the afternoon before the company announced its earnings. "We weren't exchanging inside information," said the analyst, Ivan Engel, of the hedge-fund management firm Bentley, Lamborghini & Rolls. "For crying out loud, can't a guy talk about his golf game with a friend whenever they want?"*

INSIDER, *n.* A senior executive of a company, or an external owner of at least 10 percent of a company's stock, often at least as prone to OVERCONFIDENCE as investors in general. Many insiders believe they know even more about the future of the company than they actually do. Although there is some evidence that the stocks enthusiastically purchased by top management do somewhat better than average, there are many examples of companies whose bosses bought stock heavily right up to the brink of bankruptcy.

Track the trades of insiders if you wish; but imitate them
with caution.

INSTITUTIONAL INVESTOR, *n.* Someone who,
without wise advice, is likely to ruin a large portfolio, generally $10 million or more. *See INDIVIDUAL INVESTOR.*

INTEREST, *n.* The money paid by a borrower to a
lender; the income earned by the investor in a BOND; the
attitude that an investor should vigilantly maintain toward
the financial soundness of the issuer of the bond.

The word stems from two Latin terms, *inter*, "between,"
and *esse*, "to be," and thus means "that which is, or comes,
between." It has the same origin as "interested": someone
or something that is concerned with, or brings together, a
person and an object.

The concept of interest payments is documented in one
of the world's oldest surviving legal codes, the Laws of Esh-
nunna (ca. 1900 BC). Based on the known ratios of Mesopotamian weights and measures, the interest rate on loans
of barley appears to have been 33.3 percent.

Under Roman law, *interesse* referred to the penalty due
if the debtor defaulted. Interest, in the modern sense of an
accruing rate of repayment, was known as *usura*.

In the Middle Ages, lenders were permitted by the Cath-
olic Church to book even a good loan as a kind of loss, as
the lenders had surrendered the use of the money to the borrowers, thus forgoing profit through their inability to reinvest
it. By the early 1200s, under this theory of compensation
for loss, lenders were being tacitly allowed to charge interest without being condemned for usury; the word *intereste*

begins appearing sporadically in English in the early 1300s. Interest was formally legalized in England by the statutes of Henry VIII, which set a ceiling of 10 percent interest in 1545; only after that did the word become common in English.

That rooted meaning of mutual concern passing between two parties suggests that, ideally, the one who pays interest has the same interest as the one who receives it: seeing that the entire loan is repaid on time.

INTRINSIC VALUE, *n.* What a stock is worth based on the present value of all the cash that the underlying business is expected to generate in the future, accounting for how much your money would otherwise earn in the meantime and the irreducible fact that those future cash flows are shrouded in mists of uncertainty. Because intrinsic value is only an approximation and should be stated as a range of estimates rather than as a single number, most investors prefer to focus on PRICE, which moment to moment is absolutely precise—and often wrong.

INVEST, *v.* To wrap oneself in a financial asset and hold it close; from the Latin *vestire*, to dress, clothe, wrap in robes, surround or envelop. *Investiture*, the conferring of the dignity of a formal office, usually by clothing the officer in honorary robes, has the same Latin root. There is nothing dignified about the frenzied trading of many people who call themselves "investors," however.

$ *"We're unapologetically long-term investors," said Hugo Chernus, a portfolio manager at Trott, Gallup &*

Rush, advisor to the Discretion Funds. "Unlike those high-frequency traders, we hold stocks for weeks— sometimes even months—at a time."

INVESTIGATE, *v.* What investors always should, but seldom will, do before they invest. *See also DUE DILIGENCE.*

INVESTMENT PRODUCT, *n. See PRODUCT.*

IPO, *abbr. n.* "Initial public offering," or the first sale of a company's stock by private owners who know everything about it to public buyers who know nothing about it. Marketed to the outside investors as an opportunity to get in on the ground floor of a growing business, the typical IPO instead presents the greatest opportunity to the insiders who are selling, because the associated hype enables them to cash out at inflated prices. IPO can thus more accurately be said to stand for "insiders' private opportunity," "imaginary profits only," or "it's probably overpriced."

"The Fool and His Money," Louis Dalrymple, cartoon from Puck, vol. 45 (April 26, 1899).

$ *"We can get you in on the ground floor," said Charlie Tan, a broker at Tuckett & Wendt, the investment bank leading the offering. "These guys dominate the market for integrating mobile phones into bathroom tiles, and this IPO is going to be the next Google."*

"The Blue Boat (Ship of Fools),"
Pieter van der Heyden, believed to be
after Hieronymus Bosch, engraving,
1559. Rijksmuseum

IRRATIONAL, *adj.* A word you use to describe any investor other than yourself.

IS, *v.* Has been.

When an investor or analyst says "I know that this stock is going up," what he or she means is "I know that this stock *has been* going up." That is a fact; what the stock is going to do next is conjecture.

JANUARY EFFECT, *n.* The tendency of small stocks to perform especially well in December, right before everyone buys them in January at much higher prices.

JUNK BONDS, *n.* Debt securities of less-than-investment-grade quality, now more commonly but less candidly known by the sanitized label of high-yield bonds; bought by many investors solely on the basis of the junky argument that higher income doesn't entail higher risk.

KITCHEN-SINK, *v.* To throw every conceivable bit of a company's bad news into its quarterly EARNINGS, making future comparisons more attractive; from the World War II expression for an aerial assault during which bombers drop "everything but the kitchen sink" on their targets.

In the 1980s, the term "big bath" was also common, but "kitchen sink" has since become the preferred term, perhaps because the drain of a kitchen sink tends to be clogged with such a soggy mix of unusable matter.

During the financial crisis of 2008 and 2009, many companies "kitchen-sinked the quarter" by booking the expenses of eliminating businesses and workers earlier than they otherwise would have, by recognizing the receipt of income later than they typically would have, and by acknowledging losses sooner than they normally would have. As a result, they got most of their bad news out at once, against a backdrop of terrible news for the economy overall. So, instead of being punished by investors for being incompetent and error prone, they were rewarded for appearing candid. And kitchen-sinking the results in 2009 made 2010's earnings look stellar by contrast, because profits are generally compared against the same calendar quarter one year earlier (*see* *EASY COMPS*). On Wall Street, even candor has an ulterior motive.

LEVERAGE, *n.* and *v.* Borrowed money that can amplify an investment's return or, when combined with OVER-CONFIDENCE, destroy it. From the French *lever,* to lift up, to raise; as anyone knows who has ever used a lever to move a heavy object, the force is powerful—and potentially dangerous.

When you use $500 of your own money and borrow $500, you have leveraged half of your total $1,000 investment. If its market price goes up 50 percent, you can sell it for $1,500, pay back the money you borrowed and have $1,000 left; you have doubled your money, thanks to the leverage. If, however, the market price goes down 50 percent to $500, you will be wiped out when your broker demands that you pay back the $500 you borrowed.

The lethal combination of leverage and hubris has been the fuel for every boom and bust in financial history.

See also MARGIN.

LIBOR, *abbr. n.* An acronym for London Interbank Offered Rate, an interest rate BENCHMARK used to determine how much banks pay to borrow from each other;

traditionally set by what outsiders believed was competitive bidding among banks but which turned out, in 2012, to be fraudulent collusion. Bids to set LIBOR are now under supervision of the British government and, so far at least, appear to be made fairly. Some people used to pronounce the term "LEE-bore," but now everyone knows that it is pronounced "LIE-bore."

LIQUIDATION, *n.* The forced sale of the assets of a company or individual; *liquidate* also means "to kill."

Liquidation occurs when LIQUIDITY dries up. As Joseph Conrad wrote in his great novel *Victory* (1915): "The world of finance is a mysterious world in which, incredible as the fact may appear, evaporation precedes liquidation. First the capital evaporates, then the company goes into liquidation. These are very unnatural physics."

Investors thus must be vigilant at all times to maximize their liquidity and to minimize their need for liquidation.

"*Wagon Tracks down the Dry Bed of the Colorado River,*" *Russell Lee, photograph, 1939.* LIBRARY OF CONGRESS

LIQUIDITY, *n.* A state of mind in which the owner of a financial asset believes he or she can convert it to cash at or near its market price; however, as one of Wall Street's wisest proverbs has it, "Liquidity is only there when you don't need it." So long as you want to own a security, it will be liquid; but as soon as you want to sell, it can be liquid only to the extent that everyone else doesn't want to sell it, too. That is especially true for smaller stocks, JUNK BONDS, and EMERGING MARKET securities. As the economist John Maynard Keynes warned in 1936, "There is no such thing as liquidity of investment for the community as a whole." In times of crisis, what appeared to be liquidity often turns out to be only complacency.

LOAD, *n*. In the real world, a heavy burden, often so weighty that only donkeys could carry it; on Wall Street, the sales commission on a MUTUAL FUND, ranging up to 5.75 percent of the amount invested. The two meanings are different, but only slightly.

LOCKUP, *n*. A minimum holding period, or financial prison sentence, during which hedge-fund investors may not withdraw their money. In theory, that can amplify returns by freeing fund managers from the need to sell securities into market panics, but in practice it may incarcerate investors indefinitely. "Lockup" also refers to a period—typically 90 or 180 days—during which INSIDERs are prevented from selling their shares after an IPO.

"Two Prisoners in Pillory," Delaware, photograph, ca. 1900.

LONG, *adj.* Owning an asset in the expectation, hope, or fantasy that it will rise in price; sooner or later, most people who are long find themselves longing to sell.

Also used as a noun to refer to the asset itself or the person who holds it. The more it rises in price, the harder it becomes to distinguish the long asset from the long holder—especially for the holder himself. *See also BULL.*

One of the earliest definitions of *long* is in John Russell Bartlett's *Dictionary of Americanisms* (1859): "'Long' means when a man has bought stock on time, which he can call for at any day he chooses. He is also said to be 'long,' when he holds a good deal."

There is no definitive derivation of the term *long*. It might simply have originated in the obvious image of profits lengthening as a stock's price rises over time.

LONG-TERM, *adj.* On Wall Street, a phrase used to describe a period that begins approximately thirty seconds from now and ends, at most, a few weeks from now.

 $ *"Google was a long-term holding for us," said Hugo Bailyn, a portfolio manager at Grimm, Rieper, Knight & Harkness, an investment-management firm in Opa-Locka, Florida, in an interview on June 13. "We bought it in May."*

LOSE, *v.* What happens to other investors when their assets fall in market price; it will never happen to you, of course. *See BUTTON UP; GAIN.*

LOSS AVERSION, *n.* Classical economics presumes

that people will wager an equal amount for a chance to win $100 or a chance to avoid a $100 loss. After all, either result would leave you $100 better off. Experiments by psychologists, however, have shown that people are *loss-averse:* Imagine being asked to bet on the toss of a coin. If it comes up tails, you would lose $100. How much would you have to win on heads in order to be willing to take the gamble? The typical person insists on a number between $225 and $250, showing that the pain from each dollar of loss is more than twice as intense as the pleasure from each dollar of gain.

Investors who have been "on a roll" of recent profits often forget how painful losing money is. They will soon be reminded, to their keen regret.

MAD MONEY, n. A sane way to see if you are cut out for the craziness of trading, by dedicating a discrete account exclusively to speculative bets. Much like someone who prevents himself from gambling all his money away by locking his wallet in his hotel-room safe while he brings a finite amount of cash down to the casino floor, with a "mad-money account" you put a strict limit on how much money you can commit to trading. Once you hit that maximum, you can't add any additional money to the account, no matter what.

If you make one hundred times what you put in, you will have committed enough initial capital for the final profit to make you significantly richer. But if you lose 100 percent of what you put in, your losses won't be so large that you end up significantly poorer.

See also MENTAL ACCOUNTING; SPECULATION.

MANAGEMENT, n. The people who run a company, who often are overconfident and overpaid but under the impression that they are underappreciated.

Management does matter. But research shows that if you took the CEOs with the best track records and brought them in to run the firms with the worst performance, results would improve in just 60 percent of the cases, barely better than the flip of a coin. As Warren Buffett said, "When a management with a reputation for brilliance tackles a business with a reputation for bad economics, it is the reputation of the business that remains intact."

The typical company will be much more likely to replace its CEO after a string of bad losses, and it will naturally seek to bring in its new boss from a firm that has been on a hot streak. By REGRESSION TO THE MEAN alone, the company that has been doing badly may begin to do better, and the one that was doing well may start to perform worse. That creates the dual illusion that the new CEO has fixed the company that was ailing and that his or her previous firm is falling apart now that it is run by someone else. The shareholders of the new company will naturally come to the erroneous conclusion that they have hired an indispensable leader—and will pay accordingly.

But the things a CEO can control—decisions about marketing, manufacturing, compensation, and so on—are dwarfed by the factors beyond the boss's control. The prices of raw materials, the levels of interest rates and inflation, the value of the dollar and other currencies, bursts of technological innovation, and the ebb and flow of consumers' desires for a company's products all can overwhelm any plans its management has made.

For all these reasons, the odds tend to be against investors who bet that great new management can solve bad old problems.

MARGIN, *adj., n.,* and *v.* In the real world, room for error; on Wall Street, often the cause of error. Instead of paying for a purchase outright, a trading or investing client may fund only a fraction of the cost with cash, borrowing the rest from the BROKER. The deposit serves as a *margin* to protect the broker from loss. The client, meanwhile, remains exposed to the greater risk of loss incurred by LEVERAGE.

In the nineteenth-century United States, margin on stocks was typically 10:1 ($1,000 would buy $10,000 worth of stock), sometimes as high as 20:1. Today it is typically 50 percent, meaning that you can borrow only half the market value of a financial asset. On some futures contracts, however, margin remains as high as 50:1 or even 100:1, meaning that even a tiny move in market value can wipe the client out. *See RETAIL FOREX TRADING.*

Margin trading is for experts only—and, sooner or later, will destroy many of them, too.

MARGIN OF SAFETY, *n.* The extent to which the VALUE of an underlying business exceeds the market PRICE of its securities. If the price of a company's stock falls while the value of its business remains stable, the investor's margin of safety has widened, not shrunk. Because business value changes gradually, whereas price fluctuates explosively, the margin of safety often widens in times of turmoil—meaning that investing is safest precisely when it feels riskiest. Only those who can take advantage of this paradox can reach their fullest potential as investors.

MARK, *v.* and *n.* To record the price of a security; or, if necessary, to create a price where none exists. PORTFOLIO MANAGERs often use *mark* to indicate what they think a stock or bond would be worth if they could find anyone else who wanted it. "Mark" is also a term that con men have long used to signify "victim" or "dupe," and investors who believe that a fund's "mark" on an asset is exactly what the asset is worth are themselves the biggest marks of all.

MARKET MAVEN, *n.* From the Yiddish and Hebrew *mavin*, or "understand"; someone who does not know what will happen, but who does know how to sound like someone who knows.

MARKET STRATEGIST, *n.* A direct intellectual descendant of the ancient Roman official known as a haruspex, who was practiced in the Etruscan art of divining the future by inspecting the livers of sacrificial sheep and chickens. *See also BARU.* The typical market strategist uses methods similar to those of a haruspex, but less accurate. However, the modern market strategist has much higher social status and earns vastly greater income than a haruspex, even after adjusting for more than 2,000 years of inflation.

> $ *"We're advising investors to overweight financial stocks," said Shirley Hugh-Geste, chief market strategist for Kahn, Mann, Crooke & Banditto, the Wall Street investment bank. "We think 2008 will be a record year for earnings in the financial sector as the housing sector regains its momentum."*

MARKET TIMING, *n.* The attempt to avoid losing money in BEAR MARKETs; the most common result, however, is to avoid making money in BULL MARKETs.

MATURITY, *n.* What all bonds have and what most bond traders lack.

MEMORY, *n.* An arbitrary and convenient function of the human brain enabling investors to recall all their successes and to forget all their failures.

As the great investor Benjamin Graham once remarked: "They used to say about the Bourbons [a royal dynasty of France] that they forgot nothing and they learned nothing, and [what] I'll say about the Wall Street people, typically, is that they learn nothing and they forget everything."

Investors who can remember that will be ahead of the game.

MENTAL ACCOUNTING, *n.* One more way in which the human mind refutes economic theory, in this case by arbitrarily allocating a sum of money into imaginary wallets or purses, each devoted to a different purpose. Although in theory all equal quantities of money have the same value, people often view identical sums very differently. Imagine three ways to earn $1,000: as a year-end bonus; with a winning lottery ticket; and as an inheritance from your favorite aunt. Would you spend each the same way? Of course not. You would probably use the year-end bonus to buy something useful, spend the lottery winnings on a vacation or another splurge, and invest the inheritance in something extremely safe. Where money came from, and what you intend to use it for, can often matter more in shaping your attitude toward it than how much of it you have.

"The Sack of Carthage," Georg Pencz,
engraving, 1549. Rijksmuseum

MOAT, *n.* The perceived ability of a company to defend itself against competitors and to secure a durable advantage against deterioration in profits. A moat could be a powerful brand name, such as Walt Disney; a superior design, for instance, Apple; highly competitive pricing, as with Walmart; or a dominant position within an industry, for example, Boeing. Or, as the years pass, a moat could turn out to be only a formerly powerful brand name such as Eastman Kodak; a design that used to be superior, for example, Nokia; prices that once were competitive, as with Sears Roebuck; or industrial dominance that disappeared, as with Enron.

Moats have always provided some protection from invasion, but medieval lords wisely diversified their defenses. They put iron portcullises on their front gates, stationed guards armed with crossbows atop their ramparts, and brewed up vats of Greek fire to pour down on the heads of attackers. Notwithstanding all those defenses, including a wide moat, many castles were conquered.

In the modern business world, which has so many more weapons at its disposal, competitive castles can be stormed much more easily. Although you wouldn't want to invest in a business that has no moat, you should never assume that any moat can withstand every assault. None can.

MODEL, *v.* To write complex mathematical formulas that capture every conceivable variable in every possible situation—except, that is, the one that is about to happen next, destroying the value of the portfolio that has been built around the model.

As a noun, *model* can best be defined as "a weapon of math destruction."

MO-MO, *adj.* The nickname for a MOMENTUM stock, especially those that have even mo' momentum than usual. A mo-mo stock turns instantly into an "Oh, no!" stock when its price collapses.

MOMENTUM, *adj.* and *n.* A "momentum stock" accelerates as it rises, defying the forces of friction, financial gravity, Newton's first law of motion, and logic and reason. There is no theoretical or empirical explanation of what causes momentum, why it persists (typically for two to twelve months), or why it ultimately falters. And when it ceases, a momentum stock doesn't slow down; it crashes at top speed into a brick wall, crushing any trader who still happens to own it.

All momentum traders think they can predict exactly when the stock will lose its momentum—and imagine that they can sell immediately before that. Approximately 99.999 percent of them are wrong.

MUTUAL FUND, *n.* A fund that is not mutual: its investors share all risks equally, whereas its managers share all fees exclusively.

MYOPIA, *n.* In ophthalmology, a defective condition affecting a minority of the population, in which the eye has difficulty seeing objects at a distance; also known as "nearsightedness" or "shortsightedness." As a visual defect, myopia can usually be treated with corrective lenses; therefore, few people suffer severe consequences from it. As an investing defect, however, myopia is normal and almost universal. The only known treatments are discipline, PATIENCE, and SELF-CONTROL; therefore, the majority of investors suffer severe consequences from it. *See CHURN; PORTFOLIO TURNOVER.*

NAME, *n.* A company or stock. When money managers say, "I like that name," they mean "I like that company." Note that they do not *call* it a company, which might impose the unwelcome duty of more deeply understanding the business.

In the United Kingdom, a name is someone who helps UNDERWRITE risks at Lloyd's, the insurance market in London.

NEW ECONOMY, *n.* An economy identical to the old one, with only one difference: more hype. Memes such as "new economy" are dangerous, as they seek to replace skeptical analysis with pat catchphrases. And they often proliferate at the worst possible time; Federal Reserve chairman Alan Greenspan, for instance, suggested in a speech in late 1998 that a "new economy" might well have arrived. A year and a half later, the stock-market boom he had pointed to went bust.

A "new economy" is the pretext for declaring a "NEW ERA" for investors.

Whenever someone tries to talk you into taking greater investment risk because we are in a "new economy," remember these words: "The *new* is very old; you might even say that it is the oldest thing of all." That observation comes from the diary of a wise man, the great French painter Eugène Delacroix; he jotted it down in his journal on June 8, 1850.

NEW ERA, *n.* A period of collective investing insanity during which, according to its proponents, stocks should be valued by new rules—such as "this company is growing so fast that its value is infinite." In a new era, investors no longer harbor any uncertainty about the future. The result always resembles what happened just before the Great Depression, when as Benjamin Graham and David Dodd wrote in their masterpiece, *Security Analysis*, in 1934, "The ensuing migration from business into the financial district resembled the famous gold rush to the Klondike, with the not unimportant difference that there really was gold in the Klondike."

The new era described by Graham and Dodd peaked in 1928 and 1929, but it repeated itself seven decades later.

On February 29, 2000, hedge-fund manager James J. Cramer gave a speech in which he urged investors not "to be constrained by that methodology" of trying to buy companies that have actual profits or physical assets. Money-losing but fast-growing Internet companies such as Digital Island, Exodus Communications, and Mercury Interactive, he said, were "the only ones that are going higher consistently in good days and bad." Saying that investors who seek to buy stocks valued at low multiples of their earnings or BOOK VALUE "have already gone astray," he added: "You have to throw out all of the matrices and formulas and texts that existed before the Web. You have to throw them away because they can't make money for you anymore. . . . If we use[d] any of what Graham and Dodd teach us, we wouldn't have a dime under management."

Only a few days later, the BUBBLE burst. Digital Island, which had traded at $148 per share, fell to $3.40 by the time it was taken over in May 2001; Exodus Communications went bankrupt in September 2001; Mercury Interactive's shares stopped trading on NASDAQ amid allegations of improper accounting. By the end of 2002, $10,000 invested in these new-era stocks would have been worth a grand total of $597.44.

New eras were also declared in 1720 and 1844, among many other times. There will be at least one more during your investing lifetime. When someone tells you the old rules no longer apply, remember what the great investor Sir John Templeton said: "The four most expensive words in the English language are 'This time it's different.'"

NEWS, n. Noise; the sound of chaos; the reason the prices of investments move; the lifeblood of traders; often, the bane of investors.

It is no accident that newspapers were first widely read in the coffee shops of Amsterdam and London, where crowds of overcaffeinated brokers waited to pounce on the news about (and brought by) the latest ship to arrive in the harbor.

In a series of brilliant experiments conducted in the 1980s, the psychologist Paul Andreassen found that investors who received frequent news updates on the companies in their portfolios traded roughly 20 percent more often and earned less than half as much, on average, as investors who didn't follow the news.

Keeping current on what is happening in the financial markets is not the same as knowing what will happen, as this classic front page reminds us:

Front page, New York Daily
Investment News, *October 25, 1929.*
MUSEUM OF AMERICAN FINANCE

You have no hope of succeeding as an investor unless you are well informed and cultivate your curiosity about the world. But no intelligent investor succumbs to the temptation to track the news moment to moment, every day. The financial news is like sunlight: a moderate amount is essential, but excessive exposure is dangerous and potentially fatal.

NEWSLETTER, *n.* A publication that contains no news but many letters. When the letters are formed into words claiming to predict the returns on financial assets, subscribers will usually get their money's worth, and then some. Those who paid $199 for a subscription will end up at least $199 poorer, those who paid $500 will end up at least $500 poorer, and so on.

NEXT, *adj.* In the real world, likely to appear or occur in the near future; on Wall Street, unlikely to happen at all.

Every young Internet stock with a rising price will be described as "the next Google," every two-bit conglomerate on a hot streak will be declared "the next Berkshire Hathaway," and any stock with high expectations will be christened "the next Apple."

A Google search in early 2015 for the phrase "the next Warren Buffett" turned up some 27,000 results—impressive, given that there are only about 700,000 investment advisors in the United States.

Because of REGRESSION TO THE MEAN, stocks and investment managers tend to look hottest just before they go cold. The proportion of money managers predicted to be "the next Warren Buffett" who have turned out to be even a shadow of him in the long run is approximately 0.01 percent.

As Peter Lynch, the great manager of the Fidelity Magellan Fund, wrote in his book *One Up on Wall Street*: "Another stock I'd avoid is a stock in a company that's been touted as the next IBM, the next McDonald's, the next Intel, or the next Disney, etc. In my experience the next of something almost never is—on Broadway, the best-seller list, the National Basketball Association, or Wall Street."

Ironically, after Mr. Lynch retired from active fund management, dozens of fund managers were proclaimed to be "the next Peter Lynch." None ended up amounting to a hill of beans.

Whenever you see or hear of a stock, a money manager, or any financial asset that purports to be "the next" anything, the next thing you should do is forget about it.

NIFTY FIFTY, *n.* A set of stocks believed to have almost infinite potential for growth, making investors willing to pay an almost infinite price to own them.

In the early 1970s, Morgan Guaranty Trust Co. identified fifty stocks that its clients could buy at any price and hold for any length of time. Large, stable, and fast growing, they became known as "the Nifty Fifty." Similar companies have at various times also been called glamour stocks, RELIGION STOCKs, one-decision stocks, and fancy stocks.

By the end of 1972, the average stock in the Nifty Fifty was trading at 42 times its earnings. The overall market had a P/E RATIO of 19 times, meaning that the Nifty Fifty were more than twice as expensive as stocks overall. Some were not merely expensive but exorbitant: Polaroid Corp. traded at a P/E ratio of 91 times, Avon Products at 65 times, and Xerox Corp. at 49 times.

Among the Nifty Fifty were such giants of today as Coca-Cola, General Electric, IBM, Johnson & Johnson, Procter & Gamble, and 3M. Also among them were many companies that didn't stay nifty at all: Burroughs Corp., Digital Equipment Corp., Eastman Kodak, Emery Air Freight, ITT Corp., S.S. Kresge Co., MGIC Investment Corp., J.C. Penney, Polaroid, and Jos. Schlitz Brewing Co.

By the time the bear market hit bottom in 1974, Xerox had lost 71 percent, Avon 86 percent, and Polaroid 91 percent.

The stock prices of the Nifty Fifty had been so high that they were priced as if not only the future, but the hereafter, would be glorious. A study in 2014 by Research Affiliates, an investment firm, found that if you had bought the Nifty Fifty in 1973, you would have underperformed the overall stock market for the next thirty-six years and, after four decades, would have earned an annual average of about 9.8 percent, versus around 10.4 percent if you had bought the S&P 500 index of all major stocks.

The lesson: It doesn't matter how glorious the future turns out to be if you overpaid to invest in it in the first place.

NON-TRADED REIT, n. A real-estate security that promises high income for the investor but usually delivers it only for the financial advisor. These real-estate investment trust, or REIT, shares aren't listed on a major stock exchange, may not trade for years on end, pay high apparent yields of 5 percent or more, and offer commissions of 7 percent and up to the brokers and financial planners who sell them.

Because a private REIT doesn't trade, it has no market price that can be observed fluctuating in the short run; therefore, these investments are touted as having low VOLATILITY. But a security that doesn't trade every day isn't less volatile; it is just less frequently priced. When it finally does trade, the risk that was buried within may come out with a bang after years of deceptive quiet. Many investors in non-traded REITs have suddenly lost 80 percent or more of their money after a long period of believing that their assets were stable. The high income paid by non-traded REITs will offer little comfort if most of your capital is eviscerated.

Brokers and financial planners often imply that non-traded REITs are similar to, or even good substitutes for, bonds. But with most bonds, you're assured of getting 100 percent of your principal back at maturity; with many non-traded REITs, there's no such assurance.

On average, if you play Russian roulette with a six-chambered pistol, nothing will happen five out of six times. If you think that makes Russian roulette a low-volatility hobby, you are a prime candidate for non-traded REITs.

ODD LOT, *n.* A trade of less than 100 shares of stock, traditionally regarded with contempt by the SMART MONEY that traded much larger blocks of shares than RETAIL INVESTORs could. Odd lots today, however, are dominated by INSTITUTIONAL INVESTORs, whose ALGOs break blocks of thousands of shares into tiny lots in the attempt to trade them at high speed before anyone figures out who is behind the transaction. In some stocks popular among giant investors, odd lots account for more than 60 percent of total trading volume, and at least 3 percent of all trades are in units of a single share at a time.

Until recently, trading in odd lots did not have to be reported to all market participants, although the major stock exchanges did sell information on odd-lot trades to HIGH-FREQUENCY TRADING firms that paid premium prices to the exchanges for private data feeds. Longer-term investors were thus at a disadvantage to high-speed trading firms. In December 2013, the Securities and Exchange Commission finally required odd lots to be reported to the entire market.

THE DEVIL'S FINANCIAL DICTIONARY 147

Institutional investors have effectively become the new "odd-lotters." Who, then, is the "smart money" now?

ONOCENTAUR, *n.* A creature described in ancient and medieval myths, with the torso and head of a man but the lower body of a wild ass (*onos* in Greek); also, the dominant

"A Centaur and a Female
Faun in a Landscape,"
Giovanni Domenico Tiepolo,
drawing, ca. 1775.
THE J. PAUL GETTY MUSEUM

species in modern financial markets. Seemingly rational from the waist up, but with a lower body that is lusty, wild, and dangerous, the onocentaur is ideally adapted for survival in a habitat of markets that are usually sensible but sometimes insane. The onocentaur's numbers have grown into the tens of millions. The creature's rampaging

impulses, punctuated by occasional outbreaks of good judgment, make its behavior so unpredictable that predators have only sporadic success in hunting it. Furthermore, onocentaurs can kill with a single kick, and they breed prolifically—if not constantly. These traits assure that their genes will pass on to the next generation, even though individual onocentaurs almost always die young.

OPM, *abbr. n. See OTHER PEOPLE'S MONEY.*

OPTION, *n.* The right to buy or sell a financial asset at a fixed price on or before a specific time, from the Latin *optio,*

"I choose"; a boon for stockbrokers whose clients don't understand how options work and generate a fortune in commissions as they attempt to learn.

> 💲 *Explained Hugh Askin-Mee, a client of the brokerage firm Bourne, Rich & Howe: "I put two children through Harvard by trading options. Unfortunately, they were my broker's children."*

Perhaps the earliest recorded options trade, according to Aristotle, was made by Thales of Miletus (ca. 624–547 BC), one of the "Seven Sages of Greece," who put down deposits on all nearby olive-oil presses one winter when his knowledge of astronomy purportedly told him that the next year would bring a good olive crop. Thales paid almost nothing and profited hugely when the abundant harvest created high demand for presses—thus making him one of the first individual investors to make more money trading options than his brokers did. He was also one of the last.

OTHER PEOPLE'S MONEY, *n.* Money that belongs to someone else and thus can be lost without the pain caused by losing one's own money; the term "other people's money" was popularized by future US Supreme Court justice Louis Brandeis in articles and a book of the same name published in 1913–1914. Using other people's money is even better than having a goose that lays golden eggs, he wrote, because it amounts to "taking the golden eggs laid by somebody else's goose." Today, the term is commonly abbreviated in such usages as "just OPM," "only OPM," or "nothing but OPM":

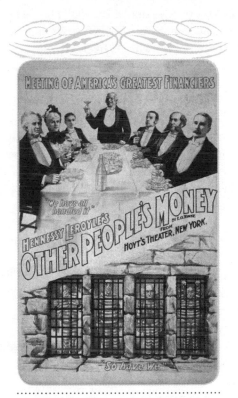

Poster for Hennessy Leroyle's
"Other People's Money," Hoyt's
Theater, New York, ca. 1900.

💲 *"Yeah, I know I lost $378 million," said Scott Free,*
an institutional trader at Hatcher, Money & Tuckett,
an investment bank in Ho-Ho-Kus, New Jersey. "But so
what? It was just OPM."

OUTLOOK, *n.* A session at the Ouija board by financial pundits; like all Wall Street FORECASTs, an outlook is an *aftercast,* based not on what is likely to happen but rather on what has been happening. If markets have been doing well lately, then the outlook will be positive; if they've been doing poorly, then the outlook will be negative.

An informal survey of market strategists by the *Wall Street Journal* in December 2006 found that nearly all had a positive outlook for 2007, without a trace of worry that a financial crisis could be on the horizon. On March 3, 2009—six days before the US stock market bottomed—the same group's forecast was abysmally pessimistic.

OVERCONFIDENCE, *n.* A belief, unjustified by the evidence, that one knows more or is better than others; the predominant personality trait of most investors and nearly every amateur trader. To be overconfident is to be ignorant of your own ignorance. In the financial markets, overcoming overconfidence is essential—and extremely expensive.

"Be Not Wise in Thine Own Eyes," Currier & Ives, lithograph, 1872. LIBRARY OF CONGRESS

OVERSIGHT, *n.* A word with two opposite meanings: "supervision," as by a regulator or risk manager, and "omission or negligence." The directly contradictory meanings should serve as a warning to investors: oversight can result in either outcome.

OVERWEIGHT, *adj.* and *v.* A larger-than-average position in a security. If Apple Inc. is 3.8 percent of the total market value of the S&P 500 stock index, for instance, then a fund that has 3.9 percent of its assets in Apple is "overweight." A portfolio manager obsessed with CAREER RISK and RELATIVE PERFORMANCE will describe that tiny difference as "a bold bet on Apple's future." *See also UNDERWEIGHT.*

PAC-MAN DEFENSE, *n.* A tactic to fend off a hostile TENDER OFFER, in which the pursued company attacks the pursuer—often saving the former in the short term and wrecking both in the long term. As in the old video game, in which a blinking dot suddenly turned ferocious and ate everything in its path, in the Pac-Man defense a company targeted in a takeover bid borrows a massive amount of money and gobbles up shares in the company that is trying to acquire it.

PANIC, *n.* and *v.* Contagious fear that sweeps across a crowd, a market, or a planet, frightening multitudes of people into selling and leaving the rest wondering whether they should. Like swarms of cicadas, long ago there were panics roughly every seventeen years, in 1819, 1837, 1857, 1873, 1893, and 1907. Less frequent in the twentieth century, panic struck twice at the onset of the new millennium: in 2000–2002 and in 2008–2009.

The word derives from the god Pan, who haunted the pastures and wild places of ancient Greece. In the form of a grinning but ugly man with the horns, ears, and hairy legs of a goat, Pan was the god of herds and flocks, serenading them with his pipes.

Fittingly, Pan was the son of Hermes, the god of shepherds, messengers, diplomacy, travel, trade, and thievery, suggesting that the relationship between panic and trade is as old as commerce itself.

Among Pan's pastimes was terrifying nymphs by chasing them through the woods. In ancient Greek art, he is often shown accompanying Dionysus, the god of wine, in a drunken Bacchana-

"Panic, as a Health Officer, Sweeping the Garbage out of Wall Street," Frank Bellew for the Daily Graphic, September 29, 1873.
LIBRARY OF CONGRESS

lia. Vases and sculptures sometimes depict Pan lugging a leather wineskin, or *bursa*, from which the modern word BOURSE is derived—another reminder of the eternal connection between panic and trade.

Pan's sweet music made him the favorite god of the gold-obsessed King Midas. Restless and untamable, Pan lurked in mountain caves and often slept at midday, arising at odd hours to race through the pastures and forests, much the way modern panics lie in wait and then burst out when markets are at their sunniest heights.

Pan also had a mischievous habit of spooking travelers by rushing at them from the forest, and city dwellers attributed nighttime squeaks and creaks to the wayward god blowing on his pipes. He was the overlord of "things that go bump in the night"—the ancestor of hobgoblins and poltergeists and the other spirits that personify the fears hiding in the recesses of the human mind.

To the Greeks, a sudden fright was called *panikos*, "of Pan." Today's herd of panicking investors, scattering in a selling frenzy set off by the unexpected, would be all too familiar to the ancient god.

Pan was also the god of fertility—and a market panic, by sweeping away the weak until bargains emerge, sets the stage for future growth. As the shrill notes of panic fade away, a calmer and quieter market tends to emerge.

Of course, once prices have risen for so long that a decline has come to seem impossible, Pan rubs the sleep from his eyes again and bursts out from his cave, his pipes blaring a tune of terror. It was ever thus, and thus it ever shall be.

PAREIDOLIA, *n.* The compulsive human tendency to see meaningful patterns or trends in random events and images. The scientist Carl Sagan suggested that pareidolia is probably an evolutionary adaptation that kept early hominids safe by enabling them to identify—and trust—the familiar. It still haunts human perception, as when people detect the Virgin Mary on a grilled-cheese sandwich, see a network of canals on the surface of Mars, perceive an old man's face on the side of a mountain, or believe that the past performance of an investment predicts its future results.

"The Old Man of the Mountain," illustration from Edwin A. Charlton's New Hampshire As It Is, 1856.

PAST, THE, *n.* In the real world, a period of time extending back years, centuries, or millennia; on Wall Street, a period of time extending back no more than five minutes ago.

The great novelist Isaac Bashevis Singer once said: "Jews suffer from many ailments, but amnesia is not among them." Wall Street suffers from many ailments also, but amnesia is foremost among them. By burying the past, the financial community can disavow any responsibility to learn from its own mistakes and can minimize the odds that its clients will be able to learn from other people's mistakes.

PATIENCE, *n.* A quality apparent among such lower life forms as snails and tortoises but rarely among humans who invest in financial assets.

Every purchase or sale of a financial asset triggers trading costs, and most incur taxes. Research has shown repeatedly that the more investors trade, the less they earn. But the urge to get rich quick is so visceral that only the most disciplined investors can cultivate enough patience to reach their goals. The others will, instead, end up getting poor quick. As Ralph Waldo Emerson wrote in his essay "Prudence": "If the hive be disturbed by rash and stupid hands, instead of honey it will yield us bees."

"Patience," Hans Sebald Beham, engraving, 1540.
RIJKSMUSEUM

P/E RATIO, *n. See PRICE/EARNINGS RATIO.*

PEER PRESSURE, *n. See HERDING.*

PERFORMANCE, *n.* A show put on to entertain the audience and gratify the egos of the performers. Long ago, and surely not by coincidence, the investment industry chose the same word to describe what it seeks to produce for its clients. Unfortunately, the members of the audience are most likely to feel entertained right before their portfolios lose a ton of money. The managers' egos, however, are unlikely to be impaired. *See also TOTAL RETURN.*

PERFORMANCE INCENTIVE FEE, *n. See FULCRUM FEE.*

PERMABEAR, *n.* An analyst, strategist, or portfolio manager who seems permanently BEARish. When, after years of a rising market, the permabears finally turn tail and become BULLish, their beliefs will become vindicated— their former beliefs, that is. Once their bearishness becomes too painful a conviction to hold, they will soon regret having let it go. Bull markets tend to die right after the last bears throw in the towel.

PERMABULL, *n.* An analyst, strategist, or portfolio manager who seems permanently BULLish. When, after years of a falling market, the permabulls finally turn tail and become BEARish, their beliefs will become vindicated—their former beliefs, that is. Once their bullishness becomes too painful a conviction to hold, they will soon

regret having let it go. Bear markets tend to die right after
the last bulls throw in the towel.

PLATE-LICKERS, *n.* The financial industry's con-
temptuous term for retirees who attend brokers' "educa-
tional" seminars and ravenously eat the free food while
sagely refusing to swallow any of the lousy investment advice
that is also on the menu.

PLUS, *adj.* Minus.
When added to the name of a MUTUAL FUND or
portfolio strategy, "plus" almost always signifies the subtrac-
tion of something from investors' results—and the addition
of higher fees by the company marketing the investment.
An "income plus" fund, for instance, typically yields income
minus losses. An "index plus" fund generally produces the
results of an index portfolio minus the toll taken by greater
risk.

POCKET, *n.* The part of your clothing through which
money will burn a hole. Benjamin Franklin reputedly used
a purse made of asbestos, which might have been financially
beneficial but is medically inadvisable.

POISON PILL, *n.* A technique by which a company
seeks to render itself toxic to a hostile bidder that submits a
TENDER OFFER, often making itself indigestible for other
investors as well. Typically, a poison pill confers upon a
company's preexisting shareholders the right to obtain more
shares at a discounted price if a hostile bidder tries to take
over, thus forcing the acquirer to pay much more money

than it intended. The failure of the takeover bid can be a bitter pill to swallow for the rest of the company's investors.

PONZI SCHEME, *n.* A fraudulent investing pitch proving that the phrase "If it sounds too good to be true, it probably is" is incorrect. If it sounds too good to be true, it definitely is. Charles Ponzi (1882–1949) in 1920 promised to double his investors' money in ninety days. In reality, he was just robbing Peter to pay Paul, showering his earliest investors with the money from his latest investors. He has had thousands of imitators and always will; the supply of people who believe that someone can work financial magic and make them rich out of the goodness of his heart is inexhaustible.

PORTFOLIO, *n.* All of an investor's financial assets—stocks, bonds, cash, and so on—regarded as a whole. Some portfolios may be able to constrain risk, but all portfolios contain it.

The word derives from the Italian *portafoglio* and the French *portefeuille*, rooted in the Latin *portare* (to carry) and *folium* (sheet or leaf), a case or folder for carrying and protecting loose papers such as legal documents or an artist's drawings; by extension, it refers to a collection of such papers, as in a student's or artist's portfolio of work. *Portfolio* does not seem to have been commonly used to describe a set of financial assets until the twentieth century.

In the Middle Ages and the Renaissance, paper was rare and valuable, so portfolios were precious objects in their own right, often made of finely decorated leather. In much the same way, a well-chosen combination of different financial assets into a portfolio gives them value and resilience they do not have in isolation; the portfolio itself is a source of protection for each of the assets within it. A good portfolio holds a wide variety of assets that don't overlap and whose prices don't vary in unison. As the Nobel laureate in economics Harry M. Markowitz proved, such an efficient portfolio reduces the uncertainty of achieving an expected return. Although it can't prevent loss, a diversified portfolio is the closest thing to a sure thing in all of finance.

PORTFOLIO MANAGER, *n.* A highly trained and even more highly compensated professional who seeks to BEAT THE MARKET by buying the best securities and avoiding the worst ones, without venturing into the kind of originality that might jeopardize his or her paycheck. With tens of thousands of portfolio managers all picking over the identical stocks and bonds with the same timid approach, outperformance is all but impossible, especially after the managers collect their fees. Portfolio managers are people who "pretend to do something they can't do and like something they don't," the great investor Charles T. Munger once said. "It's a terrible way to spend your life, but it's very well paid." *See also ACTIVE; CAREER RISK; HERDING; RELATIVE PERFORMANCE.*

PORTFOLIO TURNOVER, *n.* The buying and selling of stocks, bonds, or other securities by anyone trying to buy good investments (or those that are still cheap) and sell the bad ones (or those that are no longer cheap). In theory, the portfolio manager, investor, or trader continually removes investments with low potential and replaces them with those that have high potential. In practice, most

....
"The Juggler," from a
late-thirteenth-century
French illuminated
manuscript. THE BRITISH
LIBRARY

investors tend to hang onto their losers too long and sell their winners too soon (*see DISPOSITION EFFECT*).

Turnover is costly. Investment Technology Group estimates that it costs professional fund managers—or, rather, the *clients* of fund managers—nearly 0.5 percent to buy or sell the average US stock. A fund manager selling every stock one year after buying it is thus subtracting, on average, almost a full percentage point from the fund's annual return. (Small stocks are even more expensive; there, a fund selling its typical stock one year after buying it subtracts about 2.2 percentage points a year in trading costs.) Turnover also turns unrealized profits into realized capital gains, accelerating tax bills from the future into the present.

Turnover is meant to be a kind of lubricant that accelerates a portfolio; instead, it works more like sandpaper. The faster a portfolio manager trades, the more friction that causes, and the worse it burns. As the old saying goes, "The faster you run, the behinder you get."

The average US stock fund has a portfolio turnover rate of nearly 70 percent—nearly four times what it used to be in the 1950s and 1960s. Yet the proportion of funds beating the market has, if anything, fallen.

To translate a fund's turnover rate into a readily understandable number, divide it into 1,200. That will tell you how many months the portfolio manager holds the typical stock. Say a fund has an annualized portfolio turnover rate of 107 percent. How long does this fund hold its typical stock? Easy: 1200 ÷ 107 = 11.2 months.

Turnover often results when a portfolio manager worries that clients will wonder what they are paying him for if he just sits on their assets all year long. As Fred Schwed Jr. wrote in his classic book *Where Are the Customers' Yachts?* in 1940: "Your average Wall Streeter, faced with nothing profitable to do, does nothing for only a brief time. Then, suddenly and hysterically, he does something which turns out to be extremely unprofitable. He is not a lazy man."

Mistakes happen, and important events and new information can change the underlying values of assets. But, in general, investors who sell something soon after they bought it are probably doing something wrong. The great value investor Philip Carret liked to say that "turnover is almost indistinguishable from error." Warren Buffett's reluctance to sell is so extreme that he describes his investment style as "lethargy bordering on sloth." And as the mathematician and philosopher Blaise Pascal (1623–1662) wrote in his *Pensées*: "All the misfortunes of men come from only one thing: not knowing how to remain at rest in a room."

POTENTIAL CONFLICT OF INTEREST, *n.* An actual conflict of interest.

PRICE, *n.* A number that is often a delusion and nearly always a distraction.

The price attached to a stock or other financial asset changes in a frantic hum, often several thousand times a

day, causing corrosive intellectual damage. It may have little relation to VALUE, although it is more interesting and
keeps most of the financial media quite busy. The continual flux and spurious precision of *price* will cast an illusion
of certainty, fooling many investors into thinking that the
exact worth of a stock is knowable at any given moment.
That tricks investors into believing that even tiny changes
in price can have great significance when, in fact, the constant twitching of stock prices is nothing but statistical
noise. Under the illusion of certainty created by *price*, investors forget that *value* is approximate and that it barely
changes on even a monthly time scale. Investors who fixate
constantly on price will always end up trading too much and
overreacting to other people's mood swings; only those who
focus on ascertaining value will achieve superior returns in
the long run.

In the United States, the basic increment of stock prices
has shrunk from one-eighth (or 12.5 cents) a century ago
to the nearest penny starting in 2001; more recently, stocks
have begun to trade in tenths or even hundredths of a penny.

If asked what your house is worth, would you respond,
"Two-hundred thirty-seven thousand, four-hundred thirty-
two dollars and seventeen cents?" Of course not. You know
perfectly well that nobody, including you, knows what your
house is worth to the nearest thousand dollars, let alone to
the nearest penny or fraction of a penny. Instead, you would
say, "Between $200,000 and $250,000, maybe."

With stocks and other financial assets, price is also an
approximation; any precision is an illusion.

PRICE/EARNINGS RATIO, *n.* (*abbr.* P/E RATIO).

A company's stock price divided by its EARNINGS per share over the previous twelve months; because earnings can be manipulated in many ways and because past earnings are a poor guide to future profits, a P/E ratio is an imprecise and often misleading guide to what the company is worth. A "normalized" P/E ratio averages several years' worth of earnings to arrive at a somewhat more reliable number. A "forward" P/E relies on ANALYSTs' expectations of earnings in the coming year to arrive at a nonsensical number.

PRIME BANK, *n.* A financial scheme that is neither prime nor a bank. Prime banks are typically "based" outside the United States and "offer" current yields of 20 percent or more per month. Their offerings are typically made exclusively online, may be cloaked in breathless claims of secrecy, and are described as a combination of complex investment techniques, absolute safety, and government guarantees. But returns vastly in excess of market rates can *never* be achieved without high risk—or, in the case of prime banks, outright fraud.

PRINCIPAL, *n.* The total amount borrowed, to be repaid upon maturity; investors who lose some or all of their principal in the pursuit of YIELD have thus lost their heads.

The root word of *principal* is a combination formed in Roman times by adding *primus*, or "first," to *ceps*, an alternative form of *caput*, or "head," (from which CAPITAL is also derived). The *principal* is, then, the head of a loan—making it appropriate that investors still refer to the "face value" of a bond.

Protecting your principal is the foremost principle of FIXED-INCOME investing.

PRINT, *n*. The actual outcome, as opposed to the CON-SENSUS, or imaginary forecast. Naturally, in the world of finance the imaginary forecast matters more.

PRIVATE-EQUITY FUND, *n*. A fund that is private but not equitable, extracting massive fees from companies and often delivering mediocre results to investors. Years ago, such funds acquired companies in what were called "leveraged buyouts" using JUNK BONDS and were known as "takeover artists." Now they do "going-private transactions" using "high-yield debt" in what is called "value creation." Although the terminology has changed, the deals haven't. Nor have the fees: up to 2 percent of assets and 20 percent of profits. You could get pretty much the same financial return by using LEVERAGE to buy an INDEX FUND, but you wouldn't get the psychological return from the bragging rights of "being in private equity."

PRIVATE REIT, *n*. *See NON-TRADED REIT*.

PRO FORMA, *adj*. From the Latin for "according to form." In the real world, the term describes a perfunctory process of going through the motions. On Wall Street, it describes a different sort of motion: waving one's hands to dispel inconvenient facts such as restructuring expenses that could make a stock less desirable.

> 💲 *On a conference call with analysts yesterday, executives of Klick'n'Kitty.kom, which delivers cat litter online, were upbeat despite the company's $984 million in losses this quarter. "When you back out the restructuring*

charges, acquisition costs, and compensation expenses,
our pro-forma earnings were $203 million, up 97 percent
year-over-year," said chief financial officer Selma Sowell.
"That's what we think investors should be focusing on."

PRODUCT, *n.* A term added to the word *investment,* as
in "We've just introduced this investment product," to cloak
complexity or create the illusion of sophistication. Just as a
"wine product" is wine adulterated with water, sugar, or fruit
juice, and a "cheese product" contains such substances as
calcium phosphate, sodium alginate, and apocarotenal, so an
"investment product" often has risky additives or structural
oddities, as well as high fees, that can surprise the unwary.

   💲 *"This product is designed to provide downside protec-*
tion while still giving you plenty of upside when the stock
market does well," said Wyatt Hertz, a financial advisor
at the brokerage firm of Butcher, Cooke, Boyle, Frey &
Baker. "And, thanks to the innovative fee structure, my
interests will be aligned with yours for years to come."

See also STRUCTURED PRODUCTS.

PROFESSIONAL, *adj.* and *n.* On Wall Street, someone who acts like an amateur with other people's money.

PROFIT TAKING, *n.* A supposed wave of selling, as
in "stock prices fell amid profit taking by investors," with
the impossible implication that all the sellers are locking in
gains. (Many are selling at a loss—meaning they have no
profits to take.) Because every wave of selling must be met by

an equal and opposite wave of buying, the term *profit taking* makes no sense. *See ACT.* It is worth pondering why no one ever uses the term's natural antonym, *profit giving.* Is there none to be given?

PROMISSORY NOTE, *n.* A type of loan that promises extremely high returns, often 20 percent or more, at low risk. That promise is almost always realized in full—for the seller of the notes, not for the person who invests in them.

PROP TRADING, *n.* Shorthand for "proprietary trading," or the buying and selling of financial assets by a bank or brokerage firm on its own behalf rather than for its clients. Officially, the trades are called "proprietary" because the firm owns them. Functionally, however, the bank or brokerage firm will own only the consistently profitable trades. If the firm loses massive amounts of money on them, it could get a BAILOUT from the government, and the taxpayers would end up owning the prop trades.

The knowledge that *losing* prop trades can turn into OTHER PEOPLE'S MONEY, while *winning* trades stay proprietary, can encourage traders to take reckless risks they might otherwise avoid. Whereas economists call that "moral hazard," prop traders call it "Heads I win, tails you lose."

PROPRIETARY ALGORITHMS, *n.* Mathematical formulas ostensibly used to manage money that instead etherize the minds of prospective and current clients. The formulas often resemble something like this:

$$[([e \times R^2] / \Sigma \, i=n0)^2] \times P / b = e(R)$$

When such algorithms are algebraically reduced, they result in the simpler equation:

$$A \times f = p,$$

where A represents the assets of the firm's clients, f equals the fees they pay, and p is the gross profitability of the money-management firm (although not its clients). The other terms in the original algorithms are extraneous, although attempting to solve them does give the firm's employees something to do all day while they watch the fees piling up.

PROPRIETARY MUTUAL FUNDS, *n*. Funds that are sold by the same firm that manages them, creating what Wall Street calls a POTENTIAL CONFLICT OF INTEREST. The conflict *could* arise if the brokers working for the firm sold lots of funds managed by the same firm, and if doing so just happened to be in the best interest of the firm but not in the best interests of its clients. But that will never happen, the firm will say. Its clients might beg to differ—literally.

PROPRIETARY TRADING, *n. See PROP TRADING.*

PROSPECTUS, *n.* Chloroform for the investing mind; a legal document, dozens of pages long and numbingly boring, that enumerates every possible risk that could cause you to lose money. The tedious elaboration of risks makes them seem ordinary and dull, thus encouraging many investors to think the investment isn't risky after all. *See also*

DISCLOSURE. A prospectus should be read from back to front, as if it were printed in Arabic or Hebrew. The most dangerous risks to a company's financial health tend to be buried deep in the document, like land mines—typically in the footnotes to the financial statements or on the final pages.

PROXY STATEMENT, *n.* The annual communication in which a company requests the permission of its investors to overpay its executives for their underachievement over the previous year. Most investors throw away the proxy without reading it or voting on any of the proposals, then spend the coming year complaining about the overcompensation and underperformance of the company's managers. Every twelve months, the cycle begins anew.

PRUDENT-MAN RULE, *n.* The legal principles of good judgment under which money should be managed for other people, essentially unchanged since the early nineteenth century—although prudent men and women seem to be harder to find now than they were then. *See OTHER PEOPLE'S MONEY.*

Massachusetts Supreme Court justice Samuel Putnam wrote in 1830 that someone investing on another's behalf should "observe how men of prudence, discretion and intelligence manage their own affairs . . . considering the probable income, as well as the probable safety of the capital to be invested." Judge Putnam was ruling in a case alleging that the managers of a trust had recklessly invested in manufacturing and insurance stocks rather than in such "safe" securities as bank STOCKS or government BONDS. "It has been argued," he wrote, "that manufacturing and insurance stocks are not safe, because the principal is at hazard. But this objection applies to bank shares, as well. . . . Do what you will, the capital is at hazard."

His central point: investing is intrinsically risky. The task of the prudent man or woman is to avoid unnecessary and unrewarding risks, not all risks entirely. Prudence is the exercise of good judgment on the basis of historical evidence and careful analysis. It isn't the pursuit of safety at all costs.

PSYCHOLOGICALLY IMPORTANT, *adj.* Unimportant; trivial; nonsensical. The term *psychologically important* is often applied to "milestones" such as increments of 1,000 in the price of the Dow Jones Industrial Average or such price levels as $1,200 for gold or $100 for oil.

> $ *"We think that the Dow will go down from here," said technical analyst Connor Daley of the brokerage firm Schaefer, Shearer, Skinner, Carver & Tanner, "but it will find support at the psychologically important barrier of 18,000."*

But the stock market is not materially cheaper at 17,999.99 on the Dow than it is at 18,000.01, nor does a price of $1,200 or $100 (or any other price) indicate whether gold or oil is about to go up or down. These milestones might be psychologically important to the pundits who proclaim them so, but everyone else should regard them as meaningless.

PUMP AND DUMP, *adj.* and *v.* If you're told to "act now on this stock before it's too late," you should. Act by hanging up immediately, before it's too late. You have almost certainly just been pitched on a pump-and-dump scheme, in which a shyster buys thousands of shares of a stock, usually trading for pennies per share, and hypes it with misleading press releases, rumors, or flagrant lies. That is the pump. Then, as soon as the investing public buys into the scheme and drives up the price, the promoter sells all his or her shares at the peak and stops the hype, sending the price crashing. That is the dump.

QE, *abbr. n. See* QUANTITATIVE EASING.

QUANT, *n.* A trader or investor who relies primarily or exclusively on computer software and mathematical formulas without the noisy distractions of human judgment. The results, of course, can only be as good or bad as the judgment of the human who designed the computer software and the mathematical formulas. *See also* MODEL.

QUANTITATIVE EASING, *n.* (*abbr.* QE). The purchase of massive quantities—often hundreds of billions of dollars' worth—of bonds or other financial assets by a CENTRAL BANK in an effort to flood the financial system with money. That drives down long-term interest rates, theoretically encouraging banks to lend and investors and consumers to spend. QE has long been expected to trigger massive inflation. "The reputation of a lady is seriously endangered if she 'goes out' to get a husband instead of waiting for one," warned the conservative economist Melchior Palyi in an essay against quantitative easing in 1939. "Similarly, a

bank is not supposed to run after the customers." Palyi and
later critics have been proven wrong—so far, anyway.

QUIET PERIOD, *n.* An interval of thirty days before
a company's public offering of its securities, during which
the company provides no useful information to investors,
as opposed to all other times, when it provides almost no
useful information.

RANGE-BOUND, *adj. See SIDEWAYS MARKET.*

RATING AGENCY, *n.* A company, such as Standard & Poor's, Moody's, or Fitch, that purports to be able to tell which bonds are safer than others on a scale from AAA at best to D at the worst. After a bond DEFAULTs, rating agencies will always downgrade it if they haven't yet done so, thus forecasting with 100 percent accuracy what has already happened. History suggests that if the rating firms themselves were graded, they might well earn an F. *See also AAA; CREDIT RATING.*

REAL, *adj.* Adjusted for the ravages of INFLATION, which erodes the purchasing power of money over time. The word "real" is a useful reminder that much of the increase in the value of assets over the years is an illusion caused by inflation alone.

REAL-ESTATE INVESTMENT TRUST, *n.* (*abbr.* REIT, pronounced "reet."). A basket of companies that own commercial real estate and pass the lease payments and other income through to their investors as DIVIDENDs. Those payments are attractive, but REITs are riskier than bonds. Naturally, many brokers and financial advisors call them "bond equivalents."

REBALANCING, n. Automatically buying some of whatever has gone down and selling some of whatever has gone up. All investors say they want to buy low and sell high, which rebalancing does mechanically and unemotionally. Most investors fail to rebalance when they should, however. Buying high and selling low is much more exciting.

RED HERRING, n. In the real world, an attempt to divert attention or to confuse an issue by dragging in irrelevant information; on Wall Street, a prospectus that hasn't yet been cleared by the Securities and Exchange Commission and bears language to that effect in red ink across its cover.

Red herring are fish that have changed color after being cured in a smokehouse. More than four hundred years ago, fugitive criminals dragged smelly red herring across their escape route to throw pursuing bloodhounds off the track. Keep that image in mind whenever you read the prospectus of a contemporary stock or bond offering, and you will be on the right track.

REDEEM, v.; **REDEMPTION**, n. *The Oxford English Dictionary* defines *redemption*, from the Latin *redimere* (to buy back), as "deliverance from sin and its consequences" and "the action of freeing a prisoner, captive, or slave by payment; ransom."

In finance, you *redeem* a mutual fund when you cash out by selling it back to the company you bought it from. You may draw your own conclusions as to why the act of selling a mutual fund is described by the same word that is used to describe deliverance and salvation.

REGRESSION TO THE MEAN, *n*. The tendency of above-average results to be followed by below-average results and for unusually bad outcomes to be followed by extremely good ones; the most powerful force in financial physics.

Luck, after all, is the basic building block of which most human endeavors are made. The great value investor Benjamin Graham liked to call regression to the mean "the law of compensation" (from the Latin *compensare*, to weigh against, or to swing in the other direction).

It is difficult to predict exactly when, or by how much, events will regress to the mean; but sooner or later, in any field where luck plays a role, they always do. The inevitability of regression to the mean is denied by corporate executives, analysts, and investors—who become euphoric at the top (when they should instead grow more conservative in anticipation of the coming decline) and pessimistic at the bottom (when they should rather become more aggressive in expectation of the impending recovery). At the peak, corporate managers spend wildly on expansion, analysts project current growth rates into the distant future, and investors pay reckless prices to join the party. At the bottom, companies shut down operations that offer no immediate payoff, analysts assume business will continue to wither, and investors conclude that the Apocalypse is upon us. The crowd thus gambles that extreme events will keep getting more extreme, rather than moving in the opposite direction. By ignoring regression to the mean instead of expecting it, the crowd ends up making the effects of regression even more severe.

REGULATOR, *n.* A bureaucrat who attempts to stop rampaging elephants by brandishing feather-dusters at them. Also, a future employee of a bank, hedge fund, brokerage, investment-management firm, or financial lobbying organization. *See REVOLVING DOOR.*

The term "regulation" in the financial sense dates back at least to 1827, when Governor DeWitt Clinton told the New York state legislature in his annual message that "general regulations are indispensably necessary" to limit the risks of another banking crisis like the PANIC of 1826.

Regulation fails to stop giant financial firms from periodically destroying billions of dollars of their clients' wealth and from imperiling the global economy, but it does ensnare smaller firms in tangles of red tape that handicap their ability to compete against the larger firms. Lobbyists for giant financial firms call that "leveling the playing field."

REIT, *abbr. n. See REAL-ESTATE INVESTMENT TRUST.*

RELATIVE PERFORMANCE, *n.* How much better or worse a portfolio performs than the INDEX or BENCHMARK to which it is compared. To clients, short-term relative performance should be irrelevant, as their long-term results aren't contingent on it. To money managers, it is the only thing that matters, as their paychecks depend on it. *See also CAREER RISK.*

RELATIVE STRENGTH, n. A measure of MO-MENTUM for a stock or group of stocks, showing how much more its price has been rising lately than the market as a whole. The formula has endless variations, but in its simplest form it measures the difference in price changes over a specific period of time, say one month:

RS = (Stock price on Jan. 31 ÷ Stock price on Dec. 31) ÷ (Index price on Jan. 31 ÷ Index price on Dec. 31)

Although there is some evidence that stocks with high relative strength continue to outperform, how long that advantage will persist is controversial and unpredictable.

Because it can involve extra trading, relative strength tends to be more costly than longer-term VALUE or BUY-AND-HOLD approaches. And it often performs much worse than stocks as a whole during a BEAR MARKET. So investors should evaluate a relative-strength system with skepticism, especially if the results are based on BACKTESTing; inventing a relative-strength measure is much easier than implementing it. Numerous mutual funds have been launched ever since the 1960s to profit from relative-strength "strategies," but their own relative strength has been poor; almost none have survived.

RELIGION STOCK, n. Also known as a "one-decision stock," or shares in a company believed to be so superior that the buyer can own it forever. Because very few companies stay superior indefinitely, the market is full of people who have lost their religion. *See also NIFTY FIFTY.*

REPRESENTATIVENESS, *n.* The intuition that a small sample of data is a good representation of the population from which it is drawn, leading people to extrapolate long-term expectations from nothing more than short-term randomness.

Take H to stand for "heads," T for "tails." If you flip a coin six times, most people believe you are more likely to flip HTTHTH or THHTHT than HHHTTT or TTTHHH, although each of the four sequences is equally likely. And if your tosses produce HHHHHH or TTTTTT, onlookers will be amazed, although even longer streaks than that are common in a random process. The proper question to ask whenever an investment or a money manager is on a hot streak is not how long it has lasted, but rather how representative the results are of the probabilities of success in the long run. Short-term performance is almost never a good predictor of long-term results. Given the importance of luck, it can take fifty years or more to determine statistically whether investment performance is the product of skill or random chance. By then you—and the people who produced the performance—might no longer even be alive.

RESEARCH, *n.* The art of making financial guesswork seem like a science—at a cost to investors of approximately 1 percent of their total assets annually.

"Fundamental research" consists of pretending to study the underlying forces of supply and demand that should determine the long-term future profitability of an asset while,

THE DEVIL'S FINANCIAL DICTIONARY   179

instead, spending most of your time fixating on short-term fluctuations in market price. "Technical research" consists of looking at squiggly lines all day long.

RESISTANCE, *n*. In TECHNICAL ANALYSIS, a pattern in which the current price of an asset approaches its past high price. Even though the prices of many assets almost inevitably rise over the long term, technical analysts believe that approaching a "resistance level" somehow ensures that the price is unlikely to continue going up, at least in the short term—a period of time that the technical analyst will redefine as soon as it isn't met. *See also SUPPORT.*

RESTRUCTURING, *n*. The process by which a company that, only a few years before, had eagerly diversified into other businesses un-diversifies even more eagerly right back out of them. ANALYSTs and investors, who had earlier hailed the expansion as essential for growth, will now applaud the contraction as essential for survival. The company's management will earn big bonuses for adding to "SHAREHOLDER VALUE." A few thousand employees will lose their jobs, but that strikes the other participants as a small price to pay for restoring the company to its former state of health.

RETAIL FOREX TRADING, *n*. The rapid buying and selling of foreign-currency contracts by individuals who know nothing about foreign-currency contracts, egged on by brokerage websites and trading software that resemble a video game. The point of the video game is to lose all of your money as fast as possible, although the players don't learn that until the game is over.

RETAIL INVESTOR, *n.* Anyone who invests relatively small sums of money without earning fees or other revenue to do so; many hold their investments steadfastly through market crashes and for years or decades on end. Naturally, retail investors are derided as foolish and underperforming by the SMART MONEY and PORTFOLIO MANAGERs who rake in rich fees for delivering poor results. *See also INDIVIDUAL INVESTOR.*

RETURN ON EQUITY, *n.* (*abbr.* ROE). A measure of a company's profitability, defined as net income divided by the total investment by shareholders. Companies with a high ROE are often described as "high-quality." Unfortunately, because of REGRESSION TO THE MEAN, return on equity may often tell you more about where a company has been than about where it is going.

REVERSION TO THE MEAN, *n. See REGRESSION TO THE MEAN.*

REVOLVING DOOR, *n.* The daunting barrier that stands between REGULATORs and the industry they regulate. On one side of the barrier is at least the potential for public-spirited service to noble ideals; on the other, salaries and bonuses enabling a regulator to earn as much in a year as he or she otherwise could in a decade. Some observers nevertheless remain surprised by how fast the door can spin.

The tougher and more critical regulators are, the more money they can make when they step through the revolving door, for several reasons: (1) their toughness has earned them a reputation for objectivity, giving them credibility when they start advocating that the companies they used to restrain should now be unleashed; (2) by challenging the financial industry, they have shown that they understand how dangerous it is, earning them the respect of its leaders; and (3) the financial industry is therefore willing to pay a higher price to get them off its back. The shrewdest regulators thus tend to be hardest on the industry they regulate right before they join it. That final flourish raises their value on the open market that lies just on the other side of the revolving door.

As the widely followed financial journalist Hugh Duntz recently wrote:

> $ *This week I spoke with Eustace Seymour, a former regulator at the Securities and Exchange Commission now working as chief compliance officer for Beamer, Benz & Beamer, an investment bank in New York. "For all the criticism of 'the revolving door,' no one has ever shown that it's a problem or that it even exists at all," he said over lunch in the firm's private dining room. "The idea that a public servant would go easy on Wall Street because he might work there someday is absurd," Mr. Seymour added as he herded a few stray beads of Beluga caviar back onto his wild Scottish salmon.*

RICH, *adj*. Having as much as you want of all the things that money can't buy.

RIGHTS OFFERING, *n*. A transaction in which investors may often be deprived of their rights.

RISK, *n*. The chance that you don't know what you are doing when you think you do; the prerequisite for losing more money in a shorter period of time than you could ever have imagined possible. Risk can be formally defined

"Vanitas," Willem van Swanenburg after Abraham Bloemaert, engraving, 1611.
THE J. PAUL GETTY MUSEUM

as the odds of an adverse or undesirable outcome—when the forecast is for an 80 percent chance of sunshine, for example, then the risk of rain is 20 percent—or as the extent to which extreme outcomes differ from the average. It has been philosophically defined by finance professor Elroy Dimson of London Business School this way: "Risk means more things can happen than will happen." In the end, risk is the gap between what investors think they know and what they end up learning—about their investments, about the financial markets, and about themselves. *See also DOWNSIDE RISK; SAFE.*

RISK-AVERSE, *adj*. Not willing to take more risk—yet. When assets double or triple in price, even the most risk-averse investor will finally want to own them.

As the economic historian Charles P. Kindleberger said in his book *Manias, Panics, and Crashes*, "There is nothing so disturbing to one's well-being and judgment as to see a friend get rich."

ROGUE TRADER, n. A trader for a large bank who incurs an unauthorized loss in pursuit of an authorized risk, an event that recurs with numbing regularity, racking up hundreds of millions or billions of dollars in losses. Why do banks tolerate it? As the head of a major investment bank once said while giving a visitor a tour of his firm's trading floor, "I've got 500 traders here. I know there's [a rogue] somewhere on this floor, but if I try to rein him in, then all the other 499 will stop doing things that go right up to the edge but don't cross it, and I can't afford to bear that cost."

ROTATION, n. The mass migration of millions of speculators out of one asset whose price has just fallen and into another whose price has just risen. Because of REGRESSION TO THE MEAN, the asset that the crowd is rotating out of is soon likely to perform better than the asset that the crowd is rotating into.

Other than their complete futility, the most remarkable thing about these rotations is that they have not yet reached sufficient magnitude to worsen the subtle wobbling of the Earth's rotation around its axis—although, given the sheer number of speculators' shoes scuffling against the pavement in the same direction at any given moment, that may be only a matter of time.

"*Just a Normal Day at the Nation's Most Important Financial Institution,*" *KAL, cartoon from* Baltimore Sun, *October 17, 1989.* KEVIN "KAL" KALLAUGHER, KALTOONS.COM

RUMOR, *n.* The Wall Street equivalent of a fact.

SAFE, *adj.* A term used to promote any investment that is about to explode.

SALES LOAD, *n. See LOAD.*

SAUCER, *n.* In TECHNICAL ANALYSIS, a pattern in which prices curve downward, stay flat for a while, then slope back upward, tracing the same shape as the cross-section of a saucer. (In an "inverted saucer" pattern, stock prices first slope upward, then flatten, then turn downward.) The analysts who detect saucers in stock prices think people who see flying saucers in the sky are crazy, and perhaps they are half right about that.

SECULAR, *adj.* A series of events believed to be unfolding over the long term, from the Latin *saeculum,* an age or era; typically used to describe a TREND that is just about to end. The Japanese stock market, for example, was in a "secular bull market" until 1989, when suddenly it wasn't anymore. US stocks were in a "secular bear market" until March 9, 2009, at which point they entered a secular *bull* market—as was obvious to everyone by 2012 or so.

The antonym of secular is religious, which is what you had better be if you believe anyone can reliably identify secular trends with anything but hindsight.

See also CYCLICAL.

SECURITIZE, *v.* To bundle hundreds or thousands of assets into a single security, effectively transferring RISK from an issuer that understands it—and wants to get rid of it—to buyers who think they understand it and erroneously believe they want to own it.

In 2002, one influential expert on global finance said in a speech that securitization "has been a major contributor to the dispersion of risk in recent decades both domestically and internationally." He added, "These markets have tailored the risks associated with such assets to the preferences of a broader spectrum of investors."

In 2010, however, testimony from a leading expert took a much harsher position: Securitization, particularly of subprime mortgages, "was the immediate trigger of the current crisis."

The two opposing observations came from the same person: Alan Greenspan, chairman of the Federal Reserve Board from 1987 to 2006. He himself seems not to have understood (until the 2008–2009 financial crisis) that securitization can transfer risk efficiently and fairly only insofar as all parties to the transaction understand what they are doing. That isn't impossible, but it is mighty implausible.

SECURITY, n. A stock, bond, or other tradable financial interest in a risky asset; from the Latin *securitas*, for safety.

Among the early uses of *security* in English, dating back to at least the fifteenth century, was the meaning of property pledged by a person to ensure his or her good behavior or fulfillment of an obligation; even today, accused criminals must post security to obtain a bail bond. By the seventeenth century, that meaning had extended to the document in which a debtor promised to repay an obligation— originally a bond. Later, by analogy, it was extended to stocks and other instruments as well.

However, an investment security does not ensure that anyone will behave well, least of all the person who owns it.

SELF-CONTROL, n. The secret to success as an investor; within you lurk an angel, a devil, a scholar, and an idiot. If the angel and the scholar ever let down their guard, the devil and the idiot will wreak havoc that will take years of work to undo. Those investors who control their own behavior and abandon the futile effort to control the markets around them are the only ones who will ultimately prevail.

SELF-SERVING BIAS, n. The human tendency to attribute success to one's own actions but to blame failure on other people or uncontrollable external factors. The old saying "Success has many fathers, while failure is an orphan" has been rewritten by corporate executives and money managers as "Failure has many fathers, but success has only one: *Me*."

In their ANNUAL REPORTs, managers attribute good results to their own brilliance but blame bad outcomes on such extraneous factors as politics, wars, or the weather.

When a portfolio earns high returns, its manager will ascribe that outperformance to his or her rational, skillful selection of superior investments. The behavior of other investors, the overall environment, and luck itself have nothing to do with it.

When a portfolio performs poorly, however, the manager will attribute that to bad luck, "unprecedented events," a "difficult environment," or the bizarre behavior of all those other investors who are too irrational to appreciate the fine investments he or she has selected for you.

In early 2000, after a 26 percent gain in six months, portfolio manager Kevin Landis of the Firsthand technology funds wrote: ". . . we finished this reporting period near the top of the leader board. Like Tiger Woods, we work hard on our game. We credit our success to our research intensive investment discipline, the talent and experience of our analysts, and the expertise of our numerous industry contacts right here in Silicon Valley."

Two years later, after his main portfolio lost more than 42 percent in six months, Landis was more terse: ". . . positive economic data has yet to inspire much confidence among technology investors."

What happened to all that investment discipline, talent, and experience, and the expertise of those numerous local contacts?

SELL, *v.* What Wall Street analysts say investors should almost never do, regardless of a stock's price or market conditions. *See also BUY.*

From a recent article by the prolific financial journalist Phil DePage:

$ *Shares of EmoPhone Corp. are down 10 percent so far this year as sales of the company's leading product, an app that makes cell phones glow different colors as users' moods change, have faltered. The company's chief financial officer, Aston Martin, resigned in March amid questions about EmoPhone's accounting, which some short-sellers claim is aggressive. There is some concern that the stock, which had risen more than 35,000 percent until its recent stumble and is still valued at approximately 2,000 times the consensus forecast of what the company will earn next year, might be overpriced. Nevertheless, most analysts are optimistic. "We aren't worried, and we certainly don't think the stock is a sell," said analyst I. C. Nutton of Alfred E. Neuman & Co., a brokerage in New York.*

SHADOW BANKING, n. The supply of CREDIT by firms that aren't directly overseen by banking regulators, such as HEDGE FUNDs, finance companies, and business-development companies; called "shadow" banking because it occurs beyond the reach of the brilliant sunlight cast by the REGULATORs who foresaw and prevented the financial crisis of 2008–2009, the Asian crisis of 1998, the savings-and-loan crisis of the late 1980s, the Latin American debt crisis of 1982, and so on.

SHARE REPURCHASE, n. *See* BUYBACK.

SHAREHOLDER VALUE, n. The pretext for any potentially damaging action that a company's management takes. Sounding more elegant than "We're trying to make the price of the stock go up," *shareholder value* is invoked much more often. But it is seldom achieved. Once executives concentrate on managing the stock instead of the business, the result is all but inevitable: First the business will suffer, and then the stock will follow.

> $ *"We have honed a laser-like focus on enhancing share-holder value," said Ira Barrister, chief executive officer and chairman of Loeb Lowe Corp., the Detroit-based chain of luxury department stores. "That's why we've reduced unnecessary staff in our stores, eliminated excess marketing expenses, and borrowed $3 billion to raise the dividend and buy back stock. And that's why management and the board have bought a total of more than 200 shares of stock in the past year."*

SHEEP, *n. See* PORTFOLIO MANAGER.

SHOESHINE BOY, *n.* A reference to an anecdote about Joseph P. Kennedy, the stock manipulator who later became the first chairman of the Securities and Exchange Commission, who is said to have noted in 1929 that his shoeshine boy on Wall Street was up on the latest news about the STOCK MARKET.

"When the time comes that a shoeshine boy knows as much as I do about what is going on in the market, tells me so, and is entirely correct," Kennedy was later reported as saying, "there's something wrong with either me or the market." Kennedy promptly sold most of his stocks, the story goes, thus dodging the CRASH of 1929.

Likewise, in early 2000, the *Wall Street Journal* ran a story about William Flynn, a barber on Cape Cod in

Massachusetts, who had made more than $500,000 trading technology stocks. The image of the barber who talked about nothing but stock tips all day long came to epitomize the peak of the tech-stock BUBBLE. (Sure enough, before long the market gave the barber a bad HAIRCUT.)

And in the 1840s, as Great Britain was in the grip of railroad-stock mania, the great novelist William Makepeace Thackeray satirized the stock-trading obsession of the poor, including drunken vagrants:

> Swaggering over the stones,
> These shabby bucks did walk;
> And I went and followed those seedy ones,
> And listened to their talk.
> Was I sober or awake?
> Could I believe my ears?
> Those dismal beggars spake
> Of nothing but railroad shares.

Thackeray invented a character named James Plush, the uneducated footman of an aristocratic family in London. James starts trading with £20 and turns it almost instantly into more than £30,000, then quits his job to become a fulltime financier. He renames himself Fitz-James Augustus de la Pluche, becomes a director of forty-seven railroads, meets the king and the prime minister—and then is wiped out when the bubble bursts. He ends up working as a barkeep at the Wheel of Fortune pub. (*See FORTUNE.*)

Danger certainly rises as people who weren't previously interested in the stock market turn into avid traders. But some of Wall Street's belief in the "shoeshine boy" theory

*Shoeshine Boy, Columbus,
Georgia, John Vachon,
photograph, 1940.*
LIBRARY OF CONGRESS

is simply snobbery. If supposedly ignorant RETAIL INVESTORs are finally getting interested in stocks, then the cognoscenti can sneer even more than usual at the suckers.

But how many of those who think of themselves as SMART MONEY get out when the shoeshine boys get in? Most of the "smart money" will declare that the entry of the shoeshine boys means the bull market has further to go and there is now a bigger supply of GREATER FOOLs to sell to.

By the time the market peaks, the joke is on everyone: The people who call themselves "smart money" end up thinking like the shoeshine boys they look down upon.

SHOP, *n.* Money managers are fond of referring to their business as a "shop," as in, "Let me tell you how we do things at our shop." That creates the quaint impression that investment managers operate out of a storefront in Dickensian London, with meticulous craftsmen crouching over a workbench crafting bespoke portfolios, while customers wait at the front counter with a cup of fine tea. But there is very little handicraft in the investment business. The thing most investing "shops" are best at crafting is myths.

SHORT, *n.* and *v.* Also: **SHORTING, SHORT SALE, SHORT-SELLER,** *n.* A *short sale* involves borrowing a stock or other SECURITY, then selling it in expectation that the price will fall. The *short-seller* will then be able to purchase shares at the new, lower price and return them to the lender. The difference between the initial selling price and the subsequent purchase price is the gain from *shorting*—or the loss, if the price went up instead of down. If you get out of a short at a loss, you must COVER.

If you are LONG a security, you can't lose more than 100 percent (unless you borrowed on MARGIN). But if you are short, your losses are potentially unlimited: the asset could go up instead of down, and it could go up indefinitely.

The couplet often attributed to the stock manipulator Daniel Drew aptly describes the risk of shorting:

He that sells what isn't his'n
Must buy it back or go to prison.

Shorting has been unpopular for as long as it has existed, because investors naturally dislike anyone who tells them that their holdings might be worth less than they think. Dutch authorities attempted to prohibit short-selling several times in the seventeenth century. In his 1721 pamphlet, "The Villainy of Stock-Jobbers Detected," Daniel Defoe proposed "a Duty of 10 *per Cent.* to be paid [to] the King by the Seller" on any short sales. Sir John Barnard's Act of 1734 effectively banned short-selling—although the practice continued unabated.

The origins of the term *short* are uncertain. It might have derived from the obvious image of the price of an asset shrinking or shortening as it falls. In seventeenth-century Amsterdam, where many traders came originally from Spain, a short sale was often called *en blanco*, or a "blank," presumably because the name of the holder wasn't filled in on the transfer certificate. Perhaps, in US usage, those selling a security they didn't own were likewise "short" of the paperwork, and eventually the term became attached to the idea of the trade itself.

One of the first known usages of the term *short* is from the New York *Evening Post*, April 12, 1861, early in the Civil War, a time when selling government bonds (still sometimes called "STOCK") was viewed as unpatriotic: "When one of the members of the [New York Stock & Exchange] Board offered to sell Government Stock 'short' on time, he was instantly hissed down." The term must then have been unfamiliar to a popular audience, given that it is in quotation marks and needed the explanation "on time" (a transaction that would close later).

In his *Men and Mysteries of Wall Street*, published in 1870, James K. Medbery described short-sellers: "Believing that prices are too high, they sell, and are therefore 'short,' precisely as people who have disposed of their money are 'short' of change."

One possible derivation: in January 1856, a British court ruled on the case of *Rourke v. Short*, in which a rag dealer named Short bet another named Rourke that "a parcel of rags" was worth only half what Rourke was asking for it. The bet, which the court voided, was not strictly a short sale, as the rags didn't trade—but in principle Rourke was long, and Short was short. It is conceivable that this case, which was quoted just months later in an influential ruling in New York Superior Court, gave American speculators the snappy slang they needed to describe their bets that stocks would fall. Perhaps American traders began saying "I'm like Short," and then the phrase naturally, more evocatively, became "I'm short."

Further research on the US stock market in the 1850s and 1860s may turn up a definitive derivation for the word. In the meantime, we can only speculate about the origins of this speculative term.

SHORT-TERM, *adj.* On Wall Street, thirty seconds or less—as opposed to LONG-TERM, which is thirty seconds or more.

SIDEWAYS MARKET, *n.* A period when, instead of rising or falling, the stock market fluctuates within a narrow range. Unfortunately, sideways markets—like BULL MARKETS or BEAR MARKETS—are detectable only in hindsight. The market that has heretofore been going sideways could instantly turn upward or downward and never look back. The statement "We have been in a sideways market" may be accurate. The statement "We are in a sideways market" is not, because at any moment the sideways market might already have ended and a bull or bear market begun. *See also IS; STOCK-PICKERS' MARKET.*

SMART BETA, *n.* An INDEX (and associated INDEX FUNDs) designed not to match the market but to beat it, often by OVERWEIGHTing investments believed to offer greater VALUE and UNDERWEIGHTing those that seem to offer less. Smart beta just might work—at least for as long as most investors are too dumb to notice that it is working.

SMART MONEY, *n.* Those investors who know which stocks to buy, when to sell them, every tidbit of information that can influence the price, what the companies' executives are thinking, how geopolitical events will affect every market, and so on—as in "the smart money isn't buying yet" or "the smart money is dumping emerging-market stocks now."

No one talking about "the smart money" ever does—or could—identify exactly who these people are, however. Nor do the people who cite "the smart money" like being asked questions like these:

> If the smart money is so smart, why did it tell you what it's doing?
> If you're smart enough to know what the smart money thinks, then why aren't you keeping it a secret so you can cash in on it all by yourself?

"The smart money" is, in fact, an imaginary being, something like the many-headed hydra of Greek mythology. Cut off one of its heads and two will grow back, although both will be empty, as "the smart money" is nothing but an illusion fabricated by people who enjoy picking others' pockets.

Thus, as Peter Lynch wrote in his book *One Up on Wall Street*, "Dumb money is only dumb when it listens to the smart money."

See also THEY.

SOPHISTICATED INVESTOR, *n.* One of Wall Street's favorite oxymorons, the financial equivalent of *jumbo shrimp, military intelligence,* or *United Nations.* The term is typically used to describe a HIGH-NET-WORTH or INSTITUTIONAL INVESTOR who often deploys millions of dollars at a time. But people are not more sophisticated merely because they have more money. Often, quite the opposite is true, as their own behavior will attest. *See DUE DILIGENCE; HEDGE FUNDS.*

SPECULATE, *v.* To gamble with a SECURITY, an irony lost on most speculators, who call themselves "investors" even though they have done little or no research on the asset they are trading.

Speculation, generally buying whatever has been "hot" in the hope of finding a GREATER FOOL, is best defined by what it is not. As Benjamin Graham wrote in *Security Analysis* in 1934: "An investment operation is one which, upon thorough analysis, promises safety of principal and a satisfactory return. Operations not meeting these requirements are speculative."

STACK, *n.* The layered pile of different classes of securities that make up a company's capital, in which the odds are ultimately stacked against the holders of common stock. When all is going well, a company appears to be owned by its stockholders, who participate so generously in its growth that they often overlook the fact that they will find themselves at the bottom of the stack in case of collapse. If the company ultimately fails and goes into bankruptcy, the holders of senior debt have first claim on its assets; investors in its junior, unsecured debt come next; preferred shareholders get what's left after the junior debt holders make their claims; and common stockholders get the scraps, if any.

STOCK, *n.* The right to own a fraction of a business, re-garded by most investors as the right to play a video game.

The word "stock" is rooted in the Old Teutonic *stukko*, a stick, trunk, or log—an ancient metaphor largely forgotten as television and the Internet have reduced the idea of a stock to a TICKER SYMBOL and a stream of prices flicker-ing on a screen. A tree trunk is a solid foundation for many branches bearing green foliage and grows higher unless it is trimmed back, in which case it sprouts new growth. The history of the word *stock* thus expresses what most investors want from a stock itself—but seldom get, because they treat it like a weed rather than like a tree.

As early as AD 862, it appeared in Old English as *stocca* or *stocce*. One of its earliest meanings, by analogy to a tree trunk that generates many smaller branches, was as the source of a line of descent. That sense is still used, as in "She comes from good stock." In another early nuance, *stocke* meant a stem in which a graft, or transplanted twig, is inserted.

Early on, *stokke* referred to the wooden chopping blocks on which butchers and fishmongers hacked up their mer-chandise. In 1282, a "stokkes market" was built in the heart of the City of London; it survived until Dickens's day. A city chronicle recorded, "This yere [1450] the stokkes was dividid bitweene fishmongers and bochers [butchers]." Because Lon-don's securities market later sprang up in the same district, it is conceivable that the term *stock market* originated in this haggling, open outcry, and bloody chopping of goods into little pieces for resale.

A *stoke* or *stocke* of money appeared in English by the fifteenth century to describe a sum set aside to fund future expenses. Soon, the image of a deeply rooted core or trunk led *stock* to mean the total wealth of an individual or nation. In 1729, for instance, Jonathan Swift's *A Modest Proposal* satirically claimed that if the Irish raised babies for food, "the Nation's Stock will be thereby encreased Fifty Thousand Pounds per annum."

Stock was first used to describe the funds available for a company's operations in the early seventeenth century. "Many . . . put in different summes, which all together made up six hundred thousand pound, the first stock upon which this Company has built its prodigious Encrease," a historian of the East India Company wrote in 1669. Individual shares of that total were called *stock* as well, as were what today we call bonds.

Instead of playing with stocks as if they were blips in an electronic game, investors would be far better off planting them like trees.

STOCKBROKER, *n. See also BROKER.* A member of the purportedly extinct species *Velociraptor caveat emptor*, who in olden days charged one-time COMMISSIONs of up to 8.5 percent just to buy a mutual fund for a client. Reputed to have disappeared, they have been renamed FINANCIAL ADVISORs by the brokerage firms employing them and now typically charge a mere 1 percent every year for the rest of their clients' lives. Often, such "financial advisors" are forbidden from providing a broad range of financial advice, are under limited obligation to put their clients' interests ahead of their own, and blindly follow the recommendations of their employer regardless of their clients' circumstances. However, rechristening themselves "financial advisors" instead of "stockbrokers" has been good for business.

*Traders on the Floor of the New York
Stock Exchange, Thomas J. O'Halloran,
photograph, 1963.* LIBRARY OF CONGRESS

STOCK EXCHANGE, *n.* An organization in the business of selling information about stock prices to the highest bidder; also, a place where people trade greed and fear back and forth. *See also BOURSE; STOCK MARKET.*

STOCK MARKET, *n.* A chaotic hive of millions of people who overpay for hope and underpay for value.

The stock market serves not to allocate capital efficiently from those who have a surfeit of it to those who can put it to productive use in corporate enterprises; rather, it serves to humiliate those who think they know what the future holds. The stock market is a mechanism for putting a price tag on surprises. It transfers wealth from the arrogant to the humble, from those who trade the most to those who trade the least, from those who think they know the most to those who admit they know the least, and from those who pay commissions to those who collect them.

Those who "play" the stock market as if it were a game will lose. Those who respect it as a force of nature will prosper, but only so long as they are humble and patient.

STOCK-PICKER'S MARKET, *n*. An imaginary set of circumstances in which shrewd and skillful investors stop competing against each other and are able to trade exclusively with an unlimited supply of morons.

The justification for this belief is weak, even by Wall Street's featherweight standards of reasoning.

The vast majority of trading volume in the stock market comes from professional money managers, or "stock-pickers." So a moment's reflection should tell anyone that the term "a stock-picker's market" makes no sense. The more the market is dominated by highly paid, expertly trained, electronically equipped stock-pickers, the harder it becomes for any of them to beat the average performance of all of them.

Nevertheless, financial pundits will declare several times a year: "It's a stock-picker's market now." However, approximately two-thirds of all professional stock-pickers underperform in the typical year, regardless of how many "experts" have declared it to be a stock-picker's market.

For every stock-picker who was right to buy one stock, there must be another who was wrong to sell it; one manager's gain is always a different manager's loss. That's true whether the market is going up or down, whether some stocks are moving out of sync with others (*see* CORRELATION), or whether money is moving in or out of INDEX FUNDs. Not only is it not a stock-picker's market now, but it's never a stock-picker's market. A rare, few stock-pickers will do well in some markets; but it's impossible for most to do well at the same time.

When someone tells you "It's a stock-picker's market now," try asking "Why wasn't it before? Were the stock-pickers all picking flowers or their toes or their noses instead?"

Those who claim that "this is a stock-picker's market" should be strapped down with duct tape and forced to watch financial television on endless replay. After a few days of escalating mental anguish, such wretches will realize the error of their ways, although they might need behavioral-cognitive therapy before they can appear again in polite company.

STOP-LOSS ORDER, *n.* Also known as a "stop order" or a "stop," a trading instruction to sell a security when it falls below a certain price, which in practice may stop gains almost as reliably as it stops losses.

STRATEGY, *n.* A tactic.

In the real world of the military and in corporate management, *tactics* are short-term decisions made to implement a long-term *strategy*. But on Wall Street, "strategy" is typically a euphemism for tactics involving fast and frequent trading. The word is often a red flag indicating that someone is saying one thing and doing the opposite. So, when money managers or financial advisors are describing their "strategy," ask them, "Why do you call that a strategy instead of a tactic? What exactly makes it strategic?" They might learn something from having to answer you. You almost certainly will learn something about them.

STRUCTURED PRODUCTS, *n.* Investment PRODUCTS structured to be profitable to the firms that sell them and incomprehensible to the clients who buy them.

💲 *"This structured product couldn't be simpler," said Monty Bank, head of institutional sales at Hooke, Lyon & Singer, the global investment firm based in London. "The yield varies inversely with the magnitude of the gap between the value of Swedish krona in US dollars and the square root of the modified adjusted duration of the on-the-run twenty-year Brazilian government bond. If that goes negative, then you get LIBOR plus the yield on Apple stock divided by the value of pi. That's why we call them EZ-PIEs."*

SUPER BOWL INDICATOR, *n.* The belief that the US stock market will go up if a team from the original National Football League wins the Super Bowl championship. It is difficult to evaluate whether everyone who relies on this indicator has been hit in the helmet too many times, but there is no logical reason to believe that the performance of a multitrillion-dollar stock market over the course of the next twelve months will be determined by what happens when a couple dozen three-hundred-pound men beat the crap out of each other on a Sunday evening in February.

SUPPORT, n. In TECHNICAL ANALYSIS, a pattern in which the current price of an asset approaches its past low price. Even though the prices of all financial assets experience sharp and frequent declines, technical analysts believe that approaching a "support level" somehow ensures that the price is unlikely to continue going down, at least in the short term—a period of time that the technical analyst will redefine as soon as it isn't met. *See BOTTOM; RESISTANCE.*

Note how the term would be used by an analyst during appearances on CBUX, the popular financial television network:

> $ *"We think the gold price will find support around $1,600 an ounce," said Erin Offen, a technical analyst at the brokerage firm of Rorschach, Schmutz & Wrigglesworth in Nutley, New Jersey.—February 18, 2013 (gold price: $1,610.75)*
>
> *"Gold will find support at the psychologically important level of $1,500," said Ms. Offen. —April 7, 2013 (gold price: $1,575.00)*
>
> *"Although the $1,400 mark was pierced this week, we still think that was temporary and the support will hold," Ms. Offen said. —April 14, 2013 (gold price: $1,395.00)*
>
> *"Our indicators show that there is firm support at $1,300," Ms. Offen said. —June 17, 2013 (gold price: $1,366.75)*
>
> *"Historically, $1,200 is one of the strongest support levels for gold," said Ms. Offen. —September 28, 2014 (gold price: $1,219.50)*

The wisest investors know that the only price that is a true support level for any financial asset is zero.

SURPRISE, *n.* The sudden collision of expectations against reality; the common coin of all financial markets.

SURVIVORSHIP BIAS, *n.* An overestimate of the average past returns of financial assets or investment managers, caused by including only those that survive. As time passes and companies or asset managers go out of business, their returns disappear from many databases, making average returns appear higher in hindsight than they were in reality.

Imagine that you surveyed retired race-car drivers and found that their average age was eighty-nine. Would you therefore conclude that screeching around racetracks at 200 mph is a good way for men to prolong their lives? Of course not: Although the average age of the survivors might be high, the average lifespan of all race-car drivers, once you include those who crashed and died, is a lot shorter.

Likewise, unless the returns of the losers are counted, the long-term average performance of stocks, mutual funds, hedge funds, and the like will tend to be overstated by an average of 1 to 2 percentage points annually.

When forming expectations of the future, investors should make sure their picture of the past hasn't been distorted. History books are written by the winners, but history is produced by winners and losers alike.

SWEETEN, *v.* To raise the amount by which a company is already offering to overpay for another company it wishes to acquire.

> $ *OmniVore Corp. sweetened its bid for Nubbins Inc. by $1.50 per share today, raising its offer to $65 in cash and stock. "We think this will seal the deal," said Heidi Silver-Ware, a partner at the investment bank Bidmore Fast & Swindell, which is acting as a merger advisor to OmniVore.*

To sweeten an ACQUISITION bid makes it appear more palatable to shareholders of the target company. But, in the long run, most acquisitions barely pay off for acquirers. So any sweetening of the price may sour the shareholders of the acquiring company on any further acquisitions.

Also: **SWEETENER**, *n.*, the amount by which the acquiring company raises its bid.

SYNDICATE, *n.* In organized crime, the groups that participate in the profits from illegal activities. On Wall Street, the firms that participate in the profits from selling securities offerings. Far be it from even a cynic to suggest that the use of the identical word implies even a superficial similarity between organized crime and Wall Street.

SYNERGY, *n.* Often, the only thing one company gets when it buys another; as Warren Buffett put it, a term "widely used in business to explain an acquisition that otherwise makes no sense."

Because no one, including any of the executives at either the acquiring or the acquired company, knows what synergy is, it seldom turns out to have been worth paying for.

That, of course, doesn't prevent many people from invoking synergy to justify deals that might not otherwise seem compelling, as in this excerpt from a recent article on the website Finding Beta:

💲 *"There may be some analysts who think that a company building an amusement park in Kazakhstan has nothing in common with the startup that invented scratch-and-sniff websites," said Ken Billmore, a senior strategic organizational efficiency director at the management-consulting firm of Integrifyze 360, which advised both companies on the merger. "But they don't understand how powerful these synergies are. This is going to be a win-win-win-win situation for years to come."*

TACTICAL ASSET ALLOCATION, *n.* A way of describing "MARKET TIMING" with nine syllables instead of four, making it sound nearly two and a half times more impressive. That does not, however, make it any more likely to be successful.

TALK YOUR BOOK, *v.* For a broker, trader, or money manager, to tout or puff up your own holdings by describing them in glowing but vapid generalities. Talking one's own book is the essence of Wall Street's communications with Main Street. *See also BOOK.*

TAX SHELTER, *n.* A complicated investment that will possibly protect the investor's income from high taxes but will certainly expose it to exorbitant commissions.

TECHNICAL ANALYSIS; TECHNICAL ANALYST, *n.* A method of predicting the future prices of a financial asset by looking at its past prices, which is about as reliable as attempting to forecast tomorrow's weather by studying yesterday's. There is some evidence that technical analysis may have a weak ability to predict momentary fluctuations in price for some assets, particularly commodities and currencies. But it is unclear whether technical analysis can work over longer investing horizons. After all, the future prices of stocks and other securities are determined by the flows of cash generated by the underlying assets, not by the past prices of the securities themselves—just as the future records of sports teams are determined by how well the players perform, not by the scores of the games they played in the past.

Because the prices of securities move in an almost infinite range of patterns, no endeavor in the financial world is more encrusted with arcane jargon than technical analysis, including the HINDENBURG OMEN, Fibonacci retracements, Ichimoku clouds, vortex indicators, stochastic oscillators, triple exponential moving averages, guppy multiple moving averages, SAUCERs, stick sandwiches, double tops, triple bottoms, tweezer bottoms, HEAD AND SHOULDERS, the long-legged Doji, bearish catapults, bullish abandoned babies, the death cross, and the "upside gap two crows" pattern. It is a good general rule on Wall Street that the more impenetrable the jargon is, the less likely the thing described by it is to be profitable.

TELEVISION, *n.* A box or plane of electronic circuits that turns information into flickering images and noise—unless the information is financial, in which case it will often be turned not into noise but nonsense.

TEN-BAGGER, *n.* An investment that rises at least tenfold in price. The term was popularized by Peter Lynch, manager of the Fidelity Magellan Fund from 1977 to 1990. Lynch adapted the term from baseball, where a two-bagger is a double, a three-bagger a triple, and a four-bagger a home run. Lynch had many ten-baggers in his illustrious career; he wisely retired before they stopped coming.

TENDER OFFER, *n.* An invitation for investors to tender, or hand over, their shares to a bidder at a particular price, typically above the market price; usually there is nothing tender about such an offer. Although companies may use the technique to buy back their own shares, tender offers are more often made by hostile bidders seeking to wrest control of a company from its current management. It can take tough tactics to fend off a tender offer (*see CROWN-JEWEL DEFENSE; PAC-MAN DEFENSE; POISON PILL; WHITE KNIGHT*).

THEY and **THEM,** *pron.* The invisible powers, always referred to in a conspiratorial whisper, who supposedly move the markets. According to the people who talk about "them," they are omnipresent, omniscient, and omnipotent. Much like the three Fates of ancient Greek mythology, "they" know what will happen before it occurs and hold every investor's destiny in their hands. Yet "they" have no names, are nowhere to be found, and have no verifiable track record. Nevertheless, we are told, we should heed—and even fear—them.

As Fred Schwed Jr. wrote in his book *Where Are the Customers' Yachts?* in 1940:

*Who are "they"? They are either the great speculators
and manipulators, or the daemons of the nether world,
or both. A generation or so ago, it seems probable that
"they" had a tangible existence. . . . Then the markets
were small, and "they" were big; they played their fan-
tastic games with the price of gold or the stock of the Erie
Railroad . . . and they made and broke their followers
and each other. . . .*

*For the last ten years there haven't been any great
speculators or manipulators at all. But the use of the pro-
noun "they" continues unabated. It must be the daemons
these days, exclusively.*

Or, as "Adam Smith" wrote in his book *The Money
Game* in 1968:

*Who are They? Well, They are the people who move
stocks. They get the information first, maybe They even
create the information, and They are about to put the
stock up or down. They are mysterious, anonymous,
powerful, and They know everything. Nothing fazes
Them. They are the powers of the marketplace.*

Is there really a They?

The short answer: No, They isn't.
*See also INSIDER; SMART MONEY; SOPHISTICATED
INVESTOR.*

THRIFT, n. The obsolete practice of spending less money
than you earn; once believed to be a virtue, now regarded as
a disturbing form of deviant behavior.

TICK, *n.* A parasitic animal that can host viruses or bacteria that often inflict painful, potentially fatal neurological damage on humans; also, a single unit of change in a stock price. When markets are open for trading, those two meanings of the word may be indistinguishable.

TICKER, *n.* In the real world, slang for "heart"; on Wall Street, the machine that conveys a ceaseless stream of changing prices, the lifeblood of brokerage firms. Invented in 1867 by E. A. Calahan and refined in the following years by a young telegraph operator named Thomas Alva Edison, the ticker was a telegraph that printed the names and trading prices of stocks onto paper tape at high speed, ticking loudly as it went. Today it is computerized, flashing silently in red and green, although big moves on an electronic ticker can still produce noise when those who see it scream in joy or pain.

TICKER SYMBOL, *n.* A sequence of one to five letters representing a particular stock; the only thing that many people who call themselves "INVESTORs" know about a company.

   $ *"I just bought QHKR," said Howie Babel, a local chiropractor, to his friend Sherwood Billett, an accountant, at a recent backyard barbecue in Kokomo, Indiana. "Is that a biotech company?" asked Mr. Billett. "I don't know," answered Mr. Babel. "But it's going up, so who cares?"*

"Loves Me, Loves Me Not," cartoon from
Harper's Weekly. MUSEUM OF AMERICAN FINANCE

TIME, *n*. The novocaine of markets.

Given the passage of enough time—as little as three to five years, in most cases—the pain that a market CRASH inflicts upon investors will always dwindle. When it fades completely, another round of pain will begin.

TIP, *n*. The extreme end of a shark's fin projecting above the surface of the ocean; by visual analogy, a rumor offered to a naïve investor by someone who is either pretending to understand the market or is manipulating it.

TOP-DOWN, *adj*. Basing analytical or investing judgments on macroeconomic, geopolitical, or other forces that affect a company or a market from the outside. An investment firm whose top-down views turn out to be even temporarily profitable may be able to buy its employees Mercedes convertibles that they can all drive with the top down to remind themselves of their success. If the firm's clients heed all its future top-down forecasts too credulously, however, they may end up having to rebuild their wealth all over again, from the bottom up.

TOTAL RETURN, *n*. The full change in value of an investment, including any increases or decreases in its market price and any income, such as DIVIDENDs or INTEREST. If a stock with a 2 percent annual dividend rises 3 percent in price in a year, its total return is 5 percent. If the following year its price falls 3 percent, its total return will be –1 percent. If you have a FINANCIAL ADVISOR who points out your total return the first year, but in the second directs your attention to the dividend instead, consider getting another advisor.

Brokers Trading on the Latest News, New York Curb Exchange, photograph, ca. 1900.
MUSEUM OF AMERICAN FINANCE

Financial advisors or money managers who compare their performance to that of an INDEX will sometimes include dividends in their own returns while excluding them from the results of the benchmark. Their total return thus outperforms the partial return of the index, but that does not entitle them to say that they BEAT THE MARKET. Unless dividends are included in both numbers, these people are comparing apples to crabapples.

TOUCH, n. That certain je ne sais quoi that supposedly enabled a professional investor to appear to know how to beat the market. When that streak ends, people will say that the manager has lost his or her "touch"—although none of them would have been able to say what exactly that was while the manager was hot.

TRAILER, n. An annual fee payable to a broker for selling you a mutual fund or other investment "PRODUCT." Buy the fund once, and your broker will be paid the trailer or trailing commission, typically 0.25 percent to 1 percent, for as long as you own the fund—even if you never get another word of "advice" about it.

> $ *"I recently had a client who didn't understand trailer fees, so I explained them to her," said Caesar Bucks, a financial advisor at Fine & Seamus, a wealth-management firm in Dunstown, California. "I told her that they are a very small price to pay for our advice," he said, speaking from his boat in Catalina Bay, "and that satisfied her."*

TRANCHE, *n.* and *v.* A layer of debt with a distinctive feature or specific date of issuance, from the French for "slice" or "carve up." Some tranches may be payable sooner, some later; some may offer a stronger or weaker claim on the issuer's assets; some may pay interest in cash or in other form. Unlike the slices of a cake, however, which almost always taste good, the least-secure tranches of debt will leave a terrible taste in an investor's mouth if the issuer runs into financial trouble, as so many did in 2008 and 2009.

TREASURY, *n.* In ancient and medieval times, a storehouse where such treasures as gold, precious gems, and currency were stored for safekeeping. In modern times, a government department where gold and currency are spent, if not trashed.

TREND, *n.* The most recent set of squiggles and twitches in the continuous stream of market prices. Many online brokerage firms encourage their customers to identify and trade on "trends."

If a few consecutive squiggles go up, the market is said to be in an "uptrend," until a few of them in a row go back down, which might happen at any moment. If a few consecutive twitches go down, the market is said to be in a "downtrend," until a few of them in a row go back up, which might happen at any moment.

Trends rarely last long; neither do the amateur traders who attempt to make money from them.

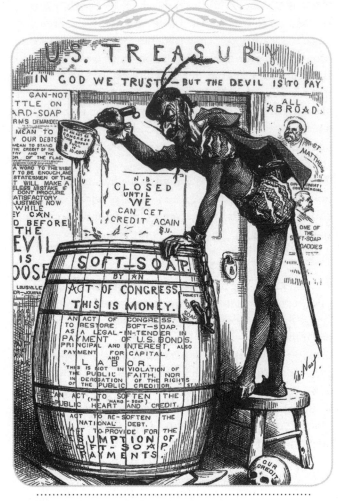

Thomas Nast, "U.S. Treasury:
'In God We Trust'—But the Devil Is to Pay."
GOOGLE IMAGES

TREND-FOLLOWING, *v.* The attempt to make money from TRENDs by following them. If you could reliably identify trends, wouldn't you be much better off anticipating them than following them? Yet the term "trend-anticipating" doesn't appear to exist in the Wall Street lexicon. Perhaps that should tell you something.

TRENDLINE, *n.* A diagonal drawn by TECHNICAL ANALYSTs, who believe it shows not only where a security's price has been but where it is going. If it ends up going somewhere else, technical analysts will draw a new trendline. It is no surprise, then, that keeping their charts up-to-date keeps technical analysts extremely busy.

$ *"So long as this trendline holds, we think the bull market has room to run," said Red Haring, a technical analyst at Chance, Gamble & Roll, a brokerage firm in Babylon, New York. "And we're getting a very strong reading that this trendline will remain intact."*

TURNOVER, *n. See* PORTFOLIO TURNOVER.

UNCERTAINTY, *n*. The most fundamental fact about human life and economic activity. In the real world, uncertainty is ubiquitous; on Wall Street, it is nonexistent. *See also CERTAINTY; VISIBILITY.*

UNCONSTRAINED BOND FUND, *n*. A mutual fund, specializing in bonds, that places no limits on the number of ways in which it can provide disappointing results to its investors. *See GO-ANYWHERE FUND.*

UNDERWEIGHT, *adj*. and *v*. A smaller-than-average position in a particular security. If Apple Inc. is 3.9 percent of the total market value of the S&P 500 stock index, for instance, then a fund that has 3.8 percent of its assets in Apple is "underweight." A portfolio manager obsessed with CAREER RISK and RELATIVE PERFORMANCE will describe that tiny difference as "a bold bet that Apple's growth is unsustainable." *See also OVERWEIGHT.*

UNDERWRITE, *v*. An investment bank *underwrites* an offering of stocks or bonds when it purchases them from the issuing company and immediately resells them to the investing public; the bank will customarily take a fee of up to 7 percent of the proceeds to compensate itself for the risk of being the sole owner of the securities for a few hours. The term comes from the historical tradition, long since abandoned, in which the partners of the banking firm signed the document that described the commitment of capital, personally *underwriting* the risk with their own names. Although underwriting risks have likely declined over the centuries, underwriting fees haven't.

UNIVERSE, *n.* The set of opportunities from which an analyst or portfolio manager can choose, inspired by the term that astrophysicists and cosmologists use to describe the totality of all energy and matter in the continuum of space and time. An investing universe, however, is much more limited—typically by the brainpower and imagination of the investor. The grandiose term "universe" cloaks the fact that, for all too many professional investors, it includes an embarrassingly narrow frame of reference and a cramped selection of potential purchases.

VALUE, *n*. A source of great confusion, as when journalists write, "The stock lost 20 percent of its value today. . . ." But it didn't lose 20 percent of its value; it lost 20 percent of its PRICE. The value of the underlying business almost certainly changed much less—if at all. Price is measured moment-to-moment; value, properly understood, unfolds over months and years. As Benjamin Graham taught Warren Buffett: "Price is what you pay, value is what you get."

Value is what an asset is worth to a sensible buyer with access to all information necessary to appraise it, based on the cash the asset is likely to generate over its life. The value of a stock depends on the cash-producing potential of the underlying business, which barely changes quarterly or monthly, let alone from day to day. The price of a stock, on the other hand, can change thousands of times in a single day even if the business of the company is utterly unaffected by any of the events that traders are reacting to.

VISIBILITY, *n*. Purported insight into or confidence about a company's future earnings, usually seen only by looking into a rearview mirror.

In late 1999 and early 2000, technology companies claimed to have "high long-term visibility" into their future earnings—and that the future was certain to be glorious. But the only visibility they had was into the past. The future (2000 through 2002) turned out to be terrible, and by 2001, technology executives were talking about "the lack of visibility"—at which point the recovery was not far off. As the economist and investing strategist Peter L. Bernstein wrote, "The future they thought was 'visible' never arrived."

Visibility, intended as a synonym for predictability, is in fact a synonym for self-delusion. There are no times when the future is more or less visible; it is always invisible.

The term dates back at least to October 1972, when Victor J. Hillery, stock-market columnist for the *Wall Street Journal*, wrote that "big high-quality companies" then possessed "what's called 'earnings visibility.'" A few months later, the crash of 1973–1974 was underway, and the earnings of even the best, highest-quality companies collapsed.

On Wall Street, myths are immutable; the only things that ever change are the names and dates.

See also CERTAINTY; UNCERTAINTY.

VOLATILITY, *n.* The extent to which an investment's short-term returns differ from its long-term average returns, technically known as *standard deviation* and colloquially known as *Oh my God!*

When an investment has been making money, the people who own it say that they are comfortable with volatility. When it starts losing money, they suddenly will declare that they hate volatility. The investment hasn't changed;

only their perceptions have. The most volatile element in financial markets is investors' own views of volatility. *See also* RISK.

Loop-the-Loop Roller Coaster,
Coney Island, New York,
photograph, ca. 1903.

WEAK HAND, *n.* In poker, a selection of cards unlikely to win. In finance, a fair-weather investor who pretends to be tough and prepared to withstand short-term loss in the pursuit of long-term gain—but who will turn out to be a coward at the first sign of trouble.

Weak hand is typically used by professional investors to indicate anyone other than themselves.

See also BONASUS.

WEALTH, *n.* A quality existing exclusively in the soul and mind that most investors erroneously believe can be measured best by the amount of money in their bank and brokerage accounts.

WEALTH MANAGER, *n.* A member of the middle class who tells members of the upper class how to manage their wealth, starting by urging them to give him or her approximately 1 percent of it every year. After many years of collecting these fees, the wealth manager will eventually become wealthy in his or her own right and might well think hard before hiring a wealth manager.

💲 *"We offer our clients access to the best asset managers and most sophisticated strategies in the world," said Kent A. Fordham, a senior partner at Chute & Killam, a wealth manager in Muttontown, New York. "The results speak for themselves," he said with a wave as he boarded his private Gulfstream jet at the nearby airport.*

WHITE KNIGHT, *n.* A bidder who comes to the rescue of a company targeted in a hostile TENDER OFFER, enabling the existing managers to believe they can keep their jobs and remain richly paid for poor performance. White knights, however, frequently turn out to have steel fists clenched inside their pale velvet gloves, and they often end up toppling the management they were brought in to rescue.

"The Archangel Michael Vanquishing the Devil," painting on glass, Dutch, ca. 1530. THE J. PAUL GETTY MUSEUM

WIDE-MOAT COMPANIES, *n. See* MOAT.

WIDOWS AND ORPHANS, *n.* The stereotypical description of investors who can't afford to take RISK but are too naïve to recognize what is risky, making them the perfect targets for financial predators.

The term "widows and orphans" referred to innocent and vulnerable investors as early as the 1820s. After the Panic of 1826, in which corrupt banking insiders fleeced the investing public, the *New York Evening Post* wrote: "Let us try to purify the atmosphere of these harpies, who practice upon the credulity of the ignorant and fatten upon the spoils of the widow and orphan." And as *Niles' Register*, a leading national newspaper, thundered: "If a *negro* steals a pair of shoes, away he must go to hard labor and solitary confinement—but if a *gentleman* violates his honor and oath, and boldly plunges into the vault of a bank, or otherwise steals and carries off 50 or 100,000 dollars belonging to widows and orphans—he rides in a coach and eats and drinks of the best, and keeps 'the best' company. There is a great deal in being a rogue of distinction!"

x, *abbr.* The symbol appearing in Internet stock quotes or newspaper stock tables indicating that a stock, mutual fund, or exchange-traded fund went EX-DIVIDEND on that day. On the ex-day or "X-date," the stock price should fall by approximately the amount of the dividend per share. Inattentive investors are often unnecessarily alarmed by that drop in price.

XBRL, *abbr. n.* A quasi-acronym for eXtensible Business Reporting Language, a coding system mandated by the US Securities and Exchange Commission—and few other organizations anywhere. Companies are thus required to convert their financial and regulatory filings from English and standard software like Excel into a computer language almost no one but the SEC can understand. The SEC then converts them back into something distantly resembling English. If those multiple steps strike you as inefficient, you don't understand how DISCLOSURE works.

YIELD, *n.* and *v.* From the ancient Indo-European *gheldh*, "to pay," a root that also survives in the modern *gelt*, or "money"; the income purportedly produced by a SECU-RITY, usually totaled over the past year, divided by its latest market price; a number that can be trumped up in countless ways to ensnare the unwary. Many investors chase yield in the pursuit of high income without ensuring first that their principal will be safe; earning a yield of 6 percent or 10 percent or more will do you no good if the investment ends up being worth much less than you paid for it. And it probably will, because extra yield is almost always a sign of extra risk. As a wise man, the late Wall Street analyst Raymond F. DeVoe, once said: "More money has been lost reaching for yield than at the point of a gun." If you buy investments for their yield alone, sooner or later you will be reminded of another ancient meaning of *yield*: to surrender or to admit defeat.

YIELD CURVE, *n.* A measure of interest rates on bonds at various maturities; predicting where the yield curve is headed is about as easy as forecasting exactly where a fistful of feathers will land in a hurricane. In a "normal" yield curve, long-term bonds pay interest at higher rates, because investors are putting their money at risk for longer periods. Yield curves can also be "flat," with interest rates relatively constant across short-term and long-term bonds; "steep," with long-term bonds having much higher yields; or "inverted," with short-term debt paying higher rates than longer-term bonds. The difficulty of prediction doesn't deter many professional bond managers from investing primarily on the basis of where they think the yield curve will be one year or more in the future. It should, however, deter you from taking them seriously.

ZOMBIE FUND, *n.* A portfolio, typically a HEDGE FUND or PRIVATE-EQUITY FUND, that functions like the living dead.

Many years after its birth, and some years after it was due to be dissolved, the fund often is left holding only vestigial assets that are difficult to price and almost impossible to sell. Its manager nonetheless charges fees as if the fund were vibrantly alive.

ACKNOWLEDGMENTS

I thank Dennis Berman, Robert Sabat, Larry Edelman, Emma Moody, and Francesco Guerrera, my editors at the *Wall Street Journal*, for tolerating this devilish enterprise. My agent, the peerless John W. Wright, inspired me at every step and even remembered having seen, in our first meeting fifteen years ago, the earliest glimmers of what became this book. John Mahaney, my editor at PublicAffairs, was the ideal sparring partner, pushing me again and again to make the book the best it could be; if I were to distill my feelings about him into a dictionary entry, the definition would consist of one word: *gratitude*. I would also like to thank the rest of the publishing team at PublicAffairs: Clive Priddle, publisher; Jaime Leifer, director of publicity; Lindsay Fradkoff, marketing director; Melissa Raymond, managing editor; Pete Garceau, who designed the cover; Pauline Brown, who created the interior design; Michele Wynn, who copyedited; and Melissa Veronesi, who skillfully managed production from final manuscript to finished book.

My friend Aravind Adiga saw the promise in this project and encouraged my obsession with it.

For providing so many of the brilliant images that brighten this book, I would also like to thank Kristin Aguilera and Sarah Buonacore of the Museum of American

Finance; Anna van Lingen and the staff of the Rijksmuseum, Amsterdam; Tom Worsdale of the US Navy; Rik Declercq and Lut De Neve of the Ghent University Library; Kristen McDonald of the Lewis Walpole Library, Yale University; and Kevin "KAL" Kallaugher, king of Kaltoons and of kindness.

My website designer, Sue Stevens of LuckyChair, provided the elegant platform for the entries that ultimately turned into this book.

Meloney Linder, Peter Kerwin, Alyson Kim, and Käri Knutson of the University of Wisconsin School of Business offered a week of hospitality in Madison exactly when I needed it most.

I shamelessly stole the joke in the OPTION entry from Michael LeBoeuf.

After I promised my wife that this book was all but finished and that the rest of the work would be "easy," she put up with far too many late nights, early mornings, and long weekends of the hard work that I still had to pour into it. As usual, she knew better.

The Wall Street Journal

JASON ZWEIG became an investment columnist for the *Wall Street Journal* in 2008. He was earlier a senior writer for *Money* and a guest columnist for *Time* and CNN.com. He is the author of *Your Money and Your Brain*, one of the first books to explore the neuroscience of investing. Zweig is also the editor of the revised edition of Benjamin Graham's *The Intelligent Investor*, the classic text that Warren Buffett has described as "by far the best book about investing ever written." Before joining *Money* in 1995, Zweig was the mutual funds editor at *Forbes*.

Zweig was for many years a trustee of the Museum of American Finance, an affiliate of the Smithsonian Institution. He serves on the editorial boards of *Financial History* magazine and the *Journal of Behavioral Finance*.